Outcomes of Education

TYRRELL BURGESS AND ELIZABETH ADAMS

Macmillan Education

First published 1980

Published by
MACMILLAN EDUCATION LIMITED
Houndmills Basingstoke Hampshire RG21 2XS
and London
Associated companies in Delhi Dublin
Hong Kong Johannesburg Lagos Melbourne
New York Singapore and Tokyo

Printed and bound in Great Britain by
Redwood Burn Ltd Trowbridge & Esher

Outcomes of Education

Contents

At 16, when compulsory education is complete, most boys and girls
gain certificates in public examinations. Unfortunately, no description
is made of what has been tested nor any statement of the young person's
unexamined competencies, attributes, interests or purposes. Because
the next stage of education and the level of employment are related to
results, examinations dominate the schools, trivialising the curriculum
and precluding young people from sharing responsibility for their own
education. Moreover, examinations are unsatisfactory as predictors of
academic success and are largely irrelevant to the needs of employers.

*Chapters 2, 3, 4 and 5 describe a number of successful innovations in assessment
practice in individual secondary schools*

In an expanding school the English Department needed to improve its
monitoring of student progress. Tackling first the reports sent to
parents, it advanced to making reports to each student. Next, students
were given access to their own files and began adding self-assessments –
and these became the cornerstone of reform in teaching, learning and
recording. The second half of the chapter stresses the point that
assessment cannot be the prerogative of teachers: self-orientation is

crucial. Details are given of the filing system needed to cope with national examiners' assessments, local teachers' assessments, and the individual students' statements.

3 Evaluation and learning in secondary schools
Jack Whitehead and Joan Whitehead

Illustrated accounts are given of how two schools, building on experience of the Schools Council's Mixed Ability in Science Project, are integrating learning with evaluation for students aged 11 to 14. In each case an extension to the 14 to 16 age group is proposed with a view to recommending a form of student profile worthy of national validation. The statements in the student profiles will be based on the moderation procedures used in 100 per cent Mode III coursework assessment in the Certificate of Secondary Education.

4 The Record of Personal Experience
Don Stansbury

A teacher who has been responsible for the design and dissemination of two systems of personally compiled records gives an instance of how these systems operate. The Record of Personal Achievement and the Record of Personal Experience, Qualities and Qualifications are built up by students in the 14 to 16 age group for use as a qualification. A case is made for making it possible for all students to compile records of this kind.

5 The Sutton Centre Profile
Colin Fletcher

From the beginning of this new community school the head and staff built up a policy concerning assessments which involved students, parents and teachers writing about and to each other. Continuous assessment throughout school life is summarised in the student's Profile. The students contribute a record of activities and compile a file of their best work. Public examination requirements are fulfilled by Mode III of the Certificate of Secondary Education. Three contemporary criticisms are, in part, answered.

Chapters 6 and 7 describe various national initiatives in instituting individual student records and profiles.

6 The Scottish Pupil Profile System
Patricia Broadfoot

Dissatisfaction with the outcomes of education in Scotland led the Head Teachers' Association there to join with the Scottish Council for Research in Education in a search for some more acceptable means of recording educational outcomes. The 'Pupil Profile', developed and evaluated with the aid of a grant from the Scottish Education Department, is described and illustrated in the chapter. The case for it is discussed in relation to the history of such reforms and current official proposals for reform from both sides of the Border regarding 16 plus.

Whereas in the UK, schools work towards public examination syllabuses recognised as having equivalence, in Europe schools often work towards nationally defined syllabuses. Recent developments in four countries are described showing that each is on the way to replacing examinations by profiles.

Denmark: the U90 Commission plans to identify general skills across four sectors of human activity: family life, leisure, working life and social life

France: the Haby Reforms (rejected) planned computerised profiles of a multiple ability concept of talent

Norway: the Norway Committee on Evaluation recommended the abolition of marks in the 7 to 16 comprehensive school. Norway seeks to reinforce control from the base. Institutional evaluation by students and teachers should increase the students' involvement and motivation

Sweden: the Report of the Commission on Marking recommended the abolition of marks in the 7 to 16 school and a Certificate to state what the student had studied and to what level. However, the 5-point scale is still used, comparability being ensured by standardised tests in most school subjects from the age of 9. Some evaluation is made of social, physical, manual and emotional development.

Chapters 8 and 9 summarise much research about assessment, records and the fulfilment of the human aims of education.

A distinction is made between summative and formative assessment. Most public examinations and school tests are summative. They are external and antipathetic to the teaching/learning process. Formative assessment is that used by students and teachers in the day to day guidance of their work. Such positive learning oriented feedback should be recognised as the commonsense meaning of 'assessment', but teachers meet many obstacles to their thinking in this way. Three case studies describing attempts to use diagnostic formative assessment in the classroom are given.

Research shows that schooling is mainly devoted to teaching and learning examinable bodies of knowledge – although both teachers and students think the aim should be to develop our most human capacities. Examinations are commonly held to be justified on the grounds of measuring general ability and predicting human potential. These claims are ill-founded. Lacking in the common formula for schooling is self-motivation – the hidden key to developing multiple human qualities such as resourcefulness, initiative and ability to learn from experience. It is proposed to switch the focus in schools from content to competence. Three techniques designed to give teachers and students credit for working towards such process goals are outlined.

An account is given of the development in a first school of internal pupil profiles. Beginning with the need to meet formal requirements, the school graduated to involving the children in their own progress, to full parental access to all school reports and towards joint decision-making between teachers and parents. Children of 5 to 8 years of age learned to reflect on their performance in language strategy tests, to comment on their abilities and their difficulties, and to choose whether or not to know what was on their records.

The Diploma of Higher Education in one polytechnic is based entirely on each student's self-assessment, stated aims, long and short term plans, and promised outcomes. The reasons for abandoning syllabuses and examinations in favour of independent study are summarised; followed by discussion and illustration of the practical procedures at the School for Independent Study. Two external boards, for validation of programmes and for assessment of outcomes respectively, give this DipHE national currency as a CNAA award.

Nationally, the Manpower Services Commission has found that few young people seeking employment have been guided or assessed in ways that enable them to get and hold down a job, or in ways that help the employer to select suitable applicants. Action research is in progress to develop an inventory of the broad-based skills found to be needed in the jobs in local areas. It is argued that the school examination system tends to create two classes, the employed and the unemployable. The knowledge and use of the inventory should bridge many gaps dividing the education system, the labour market services, employers and unions.

13 Conclusions and proposals
Elizabeth Adams and Tyrrell Burgess
Building on the experience reported in Part II, this chapter concludes
that on reaching the age of 16 every young person could have
something serious to show for his years of compulsory education: a
statement of his experience, competence, interests and purposes – to
show parents and employers alike. It offers a suggestion for the kind of
system that might be set up in a school, together with the arrangements
that could be made for gaining public recognition and support. It also
outlines national arrangements through which each school's procedures could be given a national currency. The proposals are
practicable and include the kind of organisation which would
accommodate such questions as the role of subject specialisms, the
individual tutor, the organisation of the school day, and staff/student
ratios.

Preface

JOHN TOMLINSON, *Director of Education for Cheshire, and Chairman, Schools Council*

I am very glad that Betty Adams and Tyrrell Burgess are making this attempt. I have thought for many years that we should try to make the last stages of compulsory secondary education more of a 'contract' between teachers, the pupil and, where possible, the parents also: a contract which would make explicit what each partner thought should be attempted and what he or she intended to contribute. From this it follows that the assessment and recording of what actually happens should be on a broad base; and should include elements which the parent or the pupil thought important as well as those initiated and validated solely by the school. Not only out-of-school activities but achievements in non-school clubs and private enterprise would, if the youngster chose, also be recorded. In this way would be built up not only a record of personal achievement but also a picture of interest and motivation in the round.

The educational argument for this approach seems to me unanswerable: namely, that education is in the first place about increasing general human competence, self-confidence and understanding of oneself and others. These attributes connect with the personal and social development of the young. The specific academic and practical achievements they gain depend a good deal upon that development; all too often schools make only the opposite assumption. It seems to me that schools I observe which are good for their youngsters (and therefore also good for their teachers and the community at large) have worked their way to an approach which emphasises the interaction between learning, doing practical things and human development, with the youngster as an active rather than a passive element in the process. Just as we know that the mind of a very young child grows best when it is actively engaged with the experiences it receives (rather than merely being bombarded by a kaleidoscope of un-differentiated stimuli), so I suspect that we have still to get the balance right in secondary education between formal learning (which is essential since each new human being has not got time to re-experience – or 're-discover' – everything), the kind of experience which *is* necessary because it increases resourcefulness and motivation, and an educational use of some of the reality the youngster experiences outside the school and which he is – often unconsciously and usually with mixed feelings – looking forward to when school days are finished. I simply believe that good schools use many more roads to education than do bad schools and that they keep better logs of the journeys.

I am aware that there are many hostile critics of the proposal for a record of individual achievement and all it implies for schooling. For example, they ask,

xi

won't teachers always be too generous in their assessment of the youngsters? Who would give a young man or woman starting out in life a certificate saying 'Failed-life'? But these same critics should reflect that they want life in school to be real and earnest and to prepare the young for the world of work. That world will assess them at every turn and employers will write testimonials and references as required. Indeed, many of the best employers have an annual assessment procedure in which the employee takes part and knows the assessments recorded.

I would also ask the critics to recall that it has been accepted in civilised Europe since the Greeks that the most valuable knowledge is self-knowledge. Good schools have, for centuries, tried to make people self-critical in the best sense. The self-assessment implied in helping to keep a record of personal achievement belongs to the same category. Like so much in so-called 'progressive' education, it belongs to the heart of the best historical tradition of education. The narrow and narrowing concentration on academic achievement, separated from or ignoring the development of character, is a recent development (post-1902), and an aberration.

Finally, those not convinced by these arguments might be willing to look at recent experience. I happen to have been able to observe at first hand the progress of youngsters who have entered the world of work not by the usual route but through job creation, work experience and comparable programmes. I have been struck by the way that many of them have proved so successful that the employer was willing to offer them a permanent job, although he would not have done so on the basis of their academic qualifications. Often the schools had recommended the youngster in the first place, but had nothing more tangible than their word with which to convince the employer. Had the youngster and his teachers been able to find a wider base for education and for the assessment and recording of it, perhaps the gap between what we can say we know about children after they have spent eleven years in the system and what they and their future employers need to know will be narrowed.

If this book sets more people thinking and persuades some to try things they would otherwise have ignored it will serve a valuable purpose, because secondary education in all developed countries is still searching for its soul.

Editors' acknowledgements

Our very grateful thanks are due to the contributors to this book, who not only prepared their own chapters but also came together consistently for a series of four seminars to discuss the whole question of the outcomes of education and to offer serious and sustained criticism, particularly of Parts I and III of this book.

We must acknowledge too the fact that this project would not have been possible without the sabbatical year of absence which one of us was granted by the North East London Polytechnic, and we record our gratitude to the Director and Governors.

We are grateful too to the London Business School, which made one of us a sabbatical visitor, for the opportunity to hold our seminars at the School.

We should like to acknowledge also the opportunity offered by Surrey County Council to develop, over the years, work on study groups and the use of records.

Part III of this book contains proposals for continuing action research in a number of schools. In planning this research, the editors have had the benefit of the support and guidance of a steering committee consisting of Mrs Joan Dean, Chief Inspector, Surrey County Council; Mr Peter Gorb, Senior Lecturer, London Graduate Business School; Mr Geoffrey Holland, Director, Manpower Services Commission; Professor Edmund King, King's College, University of London; Dr Desmond Nuttall, Secretary, Middlesex Regional Examining Board; Mr John Tomlinson, Director of Education, Cheshire, and Chairman, Schools Council; and Professor Sir Toby Weaver, CB.

We are most grateful for their criticism and encouragement.

The preparation of the seminars and the book itself has involved an immense amount of administrative and secretarial work, which has been undertaken by Frances Davenport and Eve Sears. We cannot thank them enough.

Finally, we are grateful to our publishers, and particularly to Martin Pick, for consistent help and interest since the project was first started. We have benefited greatly from both the encouragement and criticism we have been offered.

The editors and publishers wish to thank the Scottish Council for Research in Education for granting permission to make use of a class assessment sheet and pupil profile forms in the preparation of illustrations for Chapter 6 of this book, and also for permission to reproduce an example of a school-leaving report card.

Contributors

Elizabeth Adams, former General Inspector, Surrey County Council: *In-Service Education and Teachers' Centres* (ed.), Pergamon

Harry Black, Research Officer, Scottish Council for Research in Education, Edinburgh: *Diagnostic Assessment*, SCRE

John Blanchard, Head of English Department, Comberton Village College, Cambridgeshire

Patricia Broadfoot, Senior Lecturer in the Sociology of Education, Westhill College of Higher Education, Birmingham: *Assessment, Schools and Society*, Methuen

Tyrrell Burgess, Reader in the Philosophy of Social Institutions, North East London Polytechnic: *Education After School*, Gollancz and Penguin

Elsa Davies, Head, St Anne's First School, Stanwell, Middlesex: *The School as an Agent of Social Change*, unpublished paper

Colin Fletcher, Senior Research Fellow, Sutton-in-Ashfield Research Project, Department of Adult Education, University of Nottingham: *Issues in Community Education* (with N. T. Thompson, eds), Falmer Press

Guy Neave, Maître de Recherche, Institut d'Education FEC, Université de Paris IX Dauphine: *How They Fared: the impact of the comprehensive school upon the university*, Routledge & Kegan Paul

John Raven, Project Leader, Scottish Council for Research in Education: *Education, Values and Society: the Objectives of Education and the Nature and Development of Competence*, London, H. K. Lewis, and New York, The Psychological Corporation

Don Stansbury, Director of Studies, King Edward VI School, Totnes, Devon: *The Development of a New Curriculum Activator in Secondary Schools*, RPE Publications

John Stephenson, Head, School for Independent Study, North East London Polytechnic: 'General Competence by Independent Study' in *Report of Annual Conference*, 1977, Society for Research into Higher Education

Christina Townsend, Assistant Director of Research, Ashridge Management College, Berkhamsted, Hertfordshire: 'Post-Industrial Revolution Skills', in *BACIE Journal*, Volume 32, Numbers 7 and 9

Jack Whitehead, Lecturer, School of Education, University of Bath: *Improving Learning for 11 to 14 Year Olds in Mixed Ability Science Groups*, Wiltshire Curriculum Development Centre, Swindon

Joan Whitehead, Lecturer, Bath College of Higher Education

Introduction
Why this book was written

This book tackles one of the most serious educational problems of our time: that is, how to record and assess the outcomes of education at the end of compulsory schooling. There is widespread unease both about schooling and about educational standards. There is concern about the way standards are measured. There is growing recognition that existing or proposed examinations at 16 plus are limited both in terms of the numbers of children for whom they are apt and in terms of the range of achievement which they cover. Many students do not take the examinations; others take or pass in one or two subjects only. It is commonly assumed that those who do well are fit to enter the next stage of formal education or to take up forms of employment closed to others. Unfortunately it is not generally recognised that their success is no proof of superiority outside the limits of what was measured in the examination – largely factual knowledge, much of it trivial and irrelevant alike to the needs of the students and of society.

The problem is how to offer every young person, at the end of compulsory schooling, something to show for the years spent in school. This would need to be a positive statement of his or her abilities, attributes, interests and purposes. The problem of providing such a statement is made more difficult by the absence of agreed ways in which the outcomes of education for individuals can be recorded.

In offering a solution to this problem, this book falls into three parts. Part I is an analysis of the present inadequacy, so that the extent of the problem can be clearly understood.

The second part, which forms the bulk of the book, is a description of the progress which has been made towards a solution. It is a collection of accounts either of practice in individual schools or of the development of research in measuring and recording the outcomes of education. It concentrates upon the end of compulsory schooling but in addition draws experience both from primary schools and from further and higher education. Fortunately, in the British Isles, individual teachers and particular schools can often mount and monitor their own experiments. Moreover, as there are several separate educational systems in Britain, we have brought together material derived from Scotland as well as from

England and Wales. We have also taken into account developments in Western Europe. Taken together, Part II gives perhaps the most comprehensive outline of the evolution of good thought and practice on measurement and records at present available in Britain.

Part III takes the argument a stage further. It concludes that there is enough experience available to make possible a new system of statements for 16 year olds, nationally validated, which will more aptly meet the requirements of a public system of compulsory education. The proposals outlined here have benefited immeasurably from four seminars attended by contributors to this book at the London Graduate School of Business Studies (where Tyrrell Burgess was a sabbatical visitor in 1978). It is important to make clear, however, that individual authors are not necessarily committed to these proposals in Part III. The seminars were occasions for rigorous criticism of contributions, particularly Part III, not attempts to reach a consensus. To take only one example, Don Stansbury is campaigning for a particular solution to the problems of the 16 plus stage. He believes that there should be a system of personally compiled records for all between the ages of 14 and 16, to encourage the development of personal qualities and provide documentary evidence of them. He believes that such a system would complement a system of examinations and of reports but could not be combined with these into a single system. His system of personally compiled records would not itself require changes in the present system of examinations and reports. In other words Mr Stansbury has clear reservations about the proposals outlined in Part III.

The editors and contributors believe that a statement of pioneering practice together with feasible outline proposals for a new national system can make a particularly important contribution at this time. The present proposals for the reform of examining at 16 plus are for changes in form and organisation rather than of substance. After more than a decade of effort the reform of examinations at this stage has been found to be a dead end. Already the new Chairman of the Schools Council can contemplate publicly the possibility that these examinations might cease. It is as if the official machine is pressing for reform while recognising that general solutions must be sought elsewhere. At the same time, the schools remain under constant pressure from society and industry. Sometimes this is mediated through the political process or through agencies like the Manpower Services Commission. Sometimes it comes directly from parents or inspectors. Teachers know that they must think again if they are to meet these pressures with consistent proposals for improving the experience of their students.

This book is therefore addressed to two main groups of people. The first is that large number of head teachers and teachers in schools who have responsibility for academic organisation or who wish to promote academic change. We have sought to offer them the hope that things can be better and the confidence in themselves to make it so. Our book is not a blueprint. The examples we offer in Part II and the proposals we make in Part III are illustrative not prescriptive. We have hoped to create a framework in which individual change can take place, not to assert what that change must be. This is because we believe that education is a personal service which succeeds or fails with individuals not with systems. There are no national solutions beyond the broad provision of teachers, buildings and equipment. The answer to the problems of individual students will depend upon where they are, with whom they are working and what they are seeking to do. It is our recognition of this fact that gives our proposals their distinctive character and offers the prospect of breaking out of the stultifying effects of the last ten years of discussion.

The second group of people to whom the book is addressed includes all those who have official responsibility for the quality of education, including the Secretary of State, the inspectorate and such widely differing bodies as the Schools Council, the National Foundation for Educational Research and the Assessment of Performance Unit in the Department of Education and Science. We hope to persuade them too that there is a new approach which holds the possibility of real improvement for each student with each teacher in each school, freed from the banalities of national performance testing, core curricula, centralised initiative for curriculum development or administrative 'rationalisation'.

In short, we hope that this book will make a direct contribution not only to the development of better records and measurement but to the whole national debate about curriculum, examinations and standards. We are confident that it will stimulate thought and activity both among practising teachers and among those charged with the task of developing new systems.

Tyrrell Burgess and Elizabeth Adams
Croydon and Wimbledon, 1979

Part I
The Problem Now in Britain

1 The present inadequacy

TYRRELL BURGESS AND ELIZABETH ADAMS

In England and Wales the law places upon parents the duty to see that each child receives 'efficient full time education suitable to his age, ability and aptitude either by regular attendance at school or otherwise'. At present the age limits of compulsory education are 5 and 16 years. The central position of parents in the English education system is of great importance: it emphasises the fact that this system is a *service*. It is the means by which individual parents can fulfil the duty laid upon them by law. For most parents the duty would be impossible to fulfil unless local authorities had a corresponding duty to provide schools. At the same time as the law recognises and reinforces the natural duties of parents it also underlines the professional responsibility of teachers. 'Secular instruction' in schools, though fundamentally the responsibility of the local authorities, may be delegated to the governing bodies of individual schools, and the management, organisation and discipline of schools is a matter for head teachers. In all this, the duties of the Secretary of State for Education and Science are those of regulating and approving provision and arbitrating in disputes.

It is clear that parents can fulfil their duty by seeing that their children attend school regularly, and indeed the local authority is bound to take them to court if they fail. But this is at best a mechanical interpretation of the law. The more serious educational question is, can parents judge whether or not this regular attendance does indeed offer to the children efficient full time education suitable to their ages, abilities and aptitudes? (Very wisely the law itself offers no easy answer: it defines neither efficient nor full time, and it has little else to say about ability and aptitude.) It is our argument, and that of the contributors to this book, that if parents are to fulfil their duty and young people to understand the consequences to themselves, there must be a serious recording of the outcome of education at the end of the compulsory stage. For each individual this outcome is represented by the competencies, attributes, interests and purposes with which he or she faces the problems and opportunities of adult life. At present there is no comprehensive statement of these things with which young people leave school. Many of them leave with nothing at all to show for their years of compulsory schooling.

3

The most obvious and familiar measures are the certificates which are awarded on the basis of public examinations. The two major ones are the General Certificate of Education at Ordinary level, and the Certificate of Secondary Education. GCE O level is part of a system (which also includes the Advanced level taken usually after two further years of voluntary attendance at school) run largely by the examining boards of universities. CSE is offered by regional examining boards. Both have arrangements for seeking to secure comparability between boards. Both carry national validity. These public examinations are the only assessments which have this national validity and comparability, both of which are clearly important to young people and their parents.

On the other hand, the examinations have not been without their critics. Throughout the present century, authors of different reports have deprecated the influence of examinations on school children and teachers and have uttered pious tributes to the need for better school records. The upshot has always been the same: examinations were officially sustained and no financial or administrative support was allocated to records.

The report of the Consultative Committee of 1911 summarises the good and bad effects of examinations on the pupil and the teacher: but the School Certificate was set up in 1917 on its recommendation. By 1938 the Spens Committee was expressing disapproval of the dominance of the School Certificate on the work of the schools, 'both the framework and the content of the curriculum'. In 1943 the Norwood Report recommended radical changes in the examination system and said that in addition to a certificate of examination performance 'should be added by the school authorities an account of the pupil's school record'. In the First Report of the Secondary Schools Examinations Council published within a year or two of the 1944 Act, the enjoinder was repeated: 'Every pupil on leaving a secondary school should be provided with a comprehensive school report containing the fullest possible positive information about him and his abilities and potentialities.' Some years later the Crowther Report on the education of boys and girls between the ages of 15 and 18 said: 'Some of the purposes served by an external examination can also be met by a formal assessement by the school, at the time of leaving, of a pupil's performance and attainments during his whole time at the school. Irrespective of the growth of external examinations, we recommend that thought should be given to the development of a system of leaving certificates on these lines.'

All these quotations are derived from Appendixes to the Beloe Report, *Secondary School Examinations other than GCE*, published in 1960. Beloe himself had expressed his own caveat in his words to employers: 'Employers should bear in mind the limitations of these or any examinations as a means of recording a pupil's achievements and potentialities, and treat them as only one piece of evidence amongst others such as Heads' reports, school records and personal interviews . . . we think the usefulness of these examinations would be enhanced and some of the dangers diminished, particularly for those in the lower ranges of ability, if the examination results could be associated with arrangements for the more systematic use of school records.' The most recent statement comes from the Schools Council publication *The Whole Curriculum 13–16*. The final paragraph of this working paper reads:

'To summarise our position, we believe that what are increasingly required in the 14–16 range in the secondary school are not so much terminal measures of achievement to be used for selection purposes as kinds of assessment which provide teachers, parents and pupils with guidance. We are particularly anxious that the examination system should not perpetuate a divisive curriculum. We believe that all pupils should be offered a documentary record at the completion of their secondary schooling. This record should be a balanced account of the pupil's attainments, interests and aspirations. The document should be externally validated and underwritten by appropriately authorised bodies. We would see these bodies as offering a comprehensive assessment service which would in time supersede the present system of examining at 16 plus.'

To these traditional reservations about public examinations can be added a number of specific criticisms. In the first place they do not accommodate all 16 year olds. The evil consequences of this may have been disguised when the examinations were attempted only in selective schools to which perhaps a quarter of the children went and when most children left a year before the examination took place. Today the promise in the 1944 Act of secondary education for all is redeemed first by compulsory schooling to 16 and second by the abolition of selection at 11 for different kinds of schools. These two developments have heightened the anomaly of a system of school leaving examinations which accommodates many fewer than all school leavers.

Unfortunately the available statistics are presented in such a way as to make it hard to see what is actually happening. In the academic year 1975–6, 557000 young people left school who were aged either 15 or 16 on 1 January 1976. We call these 'young leavers' and they represented some three-quarters of the age group. Of these leavers 109 000, or nearly a fifth, left without attempting either CSE or GCE, and these figures exclude pupils in special schools. If we include those who took GCE or CSE and were ungraded then the total leaving without qualification was 132 000, or nearly a quarter.

The statistics also show those who left without 'higher grades' in CSE or GCE. The higher grades in O level are A, B and C – which are the standard of the former O level pass. (In the words of the explanatory notes to the statistics 'Grade D indicates a lower level of attainment and grade E is the lowest level of attainment judged to be of sufficient standard to be recorded'. The higher grade in CSE is grade 1, which is equivalent to a higher grade O level. In 1975–6, 226 000 young leavers left with GCE or CSE grades other than higher grades: none of these can be held to have 'passed' at GCE O level. We do not wish at this stage to comment on the quality of the courses leading to GCE or CSE. We are concerned only with the kind of recognition which young leavers get for their years at school. From this point of view the present system denies the public recognition of a 'pass' or higher grade to a total of 358 000 or well over three-fifths of all young leavers. A further 164 000 gained only four or fewer higher grades – showing that they had performed creditably (they had 'passed') in this limited range of the total curriculum. Only 46 000 received a certificate which implied substantial performance in half or more of the range of subjects taken during their compulsory schooling – one in twelve of all young leavers. Clearly the present elaborate and costly system of external examinations is not designed to inform young leavers, their parents, employers or other educational establishments about the competence of young leavers or even about the range of experience which they have had.

There are those who accept this state of affairs on the ground that it is important to maintain 'standards' and that this is done by the achievement of the minority. (It is a version of what R. H. Tawney called the tadpole philosophy: that is, the unhappy lot of tadpoles is held to be acceptable because some tadpoles do in the event become frogs.)

Unfortunately the statistics conceal the examination performance at 16 plus of those who could have left but did in fact stay on. It is these 'older leavers' (perhaps a quarter of the age group) who are usually thought to be the main beneficiaries of the system. About half of them, or a little more, generally qualify themselves for entry to higher education. It is our view, however, that existing examinations act as a selection device and do little positively for those who take them and 'pass'. They do not in themselves ensure high standards and they seriously underestimate the capacities even of those who are successful in them. They do this for two reasons. The first is that they test mostly the lowest category of performance, that of 'isolated recall' or plain memorising. They test less well the higher levels of performance like the understanding of concepts or principles, the ability to generalise or synthesise, or unfamiliar application. They do not test for example the kinds of quality, skills and attributes listed in the recent Green Paper as the aims of education: enquiring minds, respect for people, world understanding, use of language, appreciation of economic controls, mathematical and other skills, and knowledge of cultural achievements. The examinations exclude most human aptitudes and abilities, particularly those which are of most importance in managing a successful life, like persistence, courage, generosity, cooperation, human understanding.

The second reason why existing examinations underestimate the worthy is that they are tautologous. A syllabus is set and examined: success in the examination is held to indicate success in the syllabus. But there is nothing here to tell us what effect on the individual has been achieved by covering the syllabus and passing the examination. In short, what existing examinations say about intelligent and creative people is on the whole trivial and demeaning.

Nor are they much more use in helping employers to appoint young people to particular posts. It is true that employers frequently couch their requirements in terms of public examinations, giving preference to those with certificates. They do this largely because they are offered nothing else. They take success in examinations as a proxy for general ability, recognising that a young person's ability to do a job will be tested only by experience. Nor do they believe that the courses which have led to success have equipped young people for their subsequent life and work. Many assert that these courses have positively unfitted them. Educators may rightly retort that employers themselves are lax about stating clearly what qualities and competencies they in fact require – beyond an often limited statement of some technical skill – and that there is more to life than the jobs which many employers offer. But this does not absolve educators from their responsibility to find better ways than existing examinations of recording and measuring the outcome of education.

Existing examinations also have unintended consequences within the schools. Generally speaking, teachers in England and Wales claim to be in charge of what they do. There is a tradition of independence within the classroom. The internal organisation, management and discipline of the school is the responsibility of the head teacher. Local authorities have delegated to governing bodies the direction or oversight of the conduct and curriculum of the school. The authorities do not prescribe syllabuses (except for the agreed syllabuses of religious education). Still less is there any central government regulation of curricula, syllabuses or timetables. But the claims of academic freedom advanced by British teachers are held in some scorn by European educators, who are in no doubt that the British system of public examinations exercises the most powerful of external controls. It is true that schools may choose between different examining boards, so the schools at least have the freedom to choose which constraint to adopt. It is also true that one of the public examinations – the Certificate of Secondary Education – is controlled by teachers. But representation on central or regional examining bodies does not mitigate the constraint on individual schools which the examinations of these bodies impose. Our system of public examinations largely controls the curriculum as well as the internal organisation, management and discipline of secondary schools. They influence in detail the deployment of staff and their organisation in subject departments. In addition they powerfully affect the understanding of pupils of the nature of education and their confidence in themselves and its outcome.

Examinations are also used for purposes for which they are not at all apt, in particular for judging the general performance of individual teachers or schools, or the educational system as a whole over time. The annual statistics of the Department of Education and Science are constantly being mined for evidence in the debate about standards, often with a good deal of sophisticated statistical tomfoolery. But the figures of entries and passes can yield evidence only of entries and passes, not of quality or achievement either in individual pupils or of schools. What we need to know about education is the difference which a particular course or programme has made to those who have followed it. A 'good' school is one which does well by the particular children who enter it. A successful student is one who has gone far from the point at which he started. An O level grade B can be obtained for quite different performances: by the facile layabout who swots it up the night before and by the earnest plodder who transcribes notes for two years. Attempts to make general judgements about performance on the basis of such crude statements as 'grade B' are quite simply nonsensical. The temptation to do so, however, is natural with a system of national public examinations.

It is also important to remember that examinations are not cheap. They consume expensive human and material resources which would be better employed in education itself. It is impossible to discover the true cost of public examinations because much of it is represented by the time taken by teachers and students in invigilating and taking the examinations themselves, together with the preparation and organisation that the examinations require. It is not too much to say, however, that the whole of the last term of compulsory schooling is lost to education in order that public examinations may be conducted. This is too large a proportion of an adolescent's life. The direct cost is also formidable. In 1977–8 the local education authorities paid £13.5m in entrance fees for candidates in GCE O level and CSE. In the recent financial stringency, local authorities have cut back on teaching staff, on the maintenance of buildings, on books and equipment – that is on everything that might directly educate young people – while the cost of taking examinations mounts year by year (even if the rate of increase is below that of the retail price index).

Perhaps the most fundamental criticism of examinations is not so much that they are exclusive, trivial, uninformative, expensive and misused, but that they are anti-educational. They effectively preclude any sharing by the young people themselves in responsibility for their own education and for recording its outcome. Yet some such activity is essential if learning is to take place. The one thing which all the diverse and sometimes incompatible theories of learning have in common is an insistence that learning takes place through the activity of the learner. Our system of public examinations removes initiative and activity not only from the learner but also (except in CSE Mode III) from those who are most directly responsible for his learning, that is the teachers in his own school.

A suggestive experiment by Held and Hein vividly illustrates this. Two litter-mate kittens spent several hours a day in a contraption which enabled one kitten fairly normal freedom to explore its environment actively. The other was suspended passively in a 'gondola' which was moved in all directions by the movements of the exploring kitten. The gondola kitten was thus subjected to the same visual experience as the activity kitten but initiated none of the activity. When not in the contraption both kittens were kept with their mother in darkness. Tested after some weeks, the active kitten showed that it had learned to use its visual experiences for getting about (for example, by choosing the safer of two drops from a shelf) while the gondola kitten had not. Television to some extent makes gondola kittens of us all. Public examinations make gondola kittens of adolescents.

These criticisms are not at all met, indeed have scarcely been considered, by the many changes proposed in discussions in the Schools Council and elsewhere on the incidence and scope of public examinations. They have largely been concerned with ameliorating the administration of public examinations. For example, after a decade of study and research the Schools Council formulated proposals for a common system of examining at 16 plus. First codified in 1975, these are concerned rather with reducing the complexities of the work of twenty-two boards than with getting to grips with an evaluation of the system of examinations itself or with any consideration of educational alternatives. They were not accepted or rejected by the Secretary of State but became a matter for further study by the Waddell Committee which reported in July 1978, in favour of a common system.

Quite distinct from 16 plus examining is the work of the Assessment of Performance Unit, set up in 1975 with the following terms of reference: 'to promote the development of methods of assessing and monitoring the achievement of children at school, and to seek to identify the incidence of underachievement'. Ideally, the assessment model of the

APU embraces all the important lines of child development, and already the scope of the work in hand goes far beyond what has been previously attempted. Advances were made first in assessing mathematics, scientific development and various forms of language development, while problems of assessment in aesthetics, in physical development and in personal and social development are all meant to be tackled.

Compared with 16 plus examinations (not to speak of 11 plus examinations), these APU studies represent a broadening and deepening of the concept of what, in school education, is capable of being monitored and assessed. The APU monitoring procedure is so designed that the results for individual students, schools or even LEAs will not be identifiable. It is intended to conduct testing on a small percentage of particular age groups and not to submit any individual child to the rigours of a full test. By such means the APU aims to produce facts and figures about national standards in schools.

Unfortunately, as with other examining, the aims and the consequences may not coincide. The danger is that once published, APU-type test materials will be available for less legitimate purposes than those of the national body. If the actual APU material is withheld – as promised – comparable tests based on item banks will be available. Some local education authorities are already planning saturation testing of children in the schools in their areas. Not all these LEAs will be able to resist the temptation to publish results – perhaps because few administrators and fewer politicians recognise the crass unfairness of such league tables and the incalculable harm done to students, teachers and whole communities by crude comparison of the results of tests.

The pity of all this is that it ignores the recent experience in British schools of shifting responsibility for education and its outcome through different levels. At the first level teachers and students work to external syllabuses. In the second teachers take responsibility for the curriculum themselves, and in the third the relationship of student and teacher is one in which each helps the youngster to make something of his own life. It is worth outlining some of the progress which gives ground for hope.

We begin with the first level, where teachers work to external syllabuses and requirements and students are similarly denied effective choice and the exercise of responsibility. This picture, of teachers obeying instructions and of students being expected similarly to fall into line, was general in secondary as well as in elementary schools prior to the 1944 Education Act. It remains characteristic of large parts of the world today. The passing of the 1944 Act, with the promise of secondary education for all, the raising of the school leaving age to 15 and later to 16, and the change to comprehensive secondary education have all resulted in a tendency for the proportion of examined 16 year olds to increase and for that of the non-examined to drop. Within each school, of course, differentiation into examined and non-examined students continues to dominate the ethos and the procedures.

The introduction of the Certificate of Secondary Education in the 1960s, following the Beloe Report, has been important not only in trebling the proportion of candidates at 16 plus, but also in introducing teacher control of school examinations. In the event, the Beloe recommendation about teacher control meant that in each of fourteen regions covering England and Wales, secondary teachers, linked by subject interest, had to accept responsibility for preparing syllabuses, setting papers, assessing standards and monitoring comparability of courses and entries for public examinations affecting perhaps half the 16 plus age group. Their work was supported from the outset by an adequate administrative structure located in offices outside the control of any single local authority or university examining board.

Two further reports confirmed this trend. Like the Beloe Report, the Newsom and the Lockwood Reports were both published in the early 1960s. Newsom focused attention on that half of the nation's future, as he named it, which until that time had received little official interest: the students of average and less than average ability. His recommendations helped to legitimate some of the tentative efforts teachers had been making to relate school and out of school activities to student needs and interests. The Lockwood Report led to the setting up of the national Schools Council for Curriculum and Examinations, an independent body with a majority of teacher members. Its avowed purpose was: 'to undertake research and development work in curricula, teaching methods and examinations in schools, and in other ways to help teachers decide what to teach and how. In all its work it had regard to the general principle . . . that each school should have the fullest possible measure of responsibility for its own work with its own curriculum and teaching methods based on the needs of its own pupils and evolved by its own staff.'

The effect of these three reports was to provide teachers with ideas about curriculum and teaching methods as well as with new responsibilities for conducting examinations. Within a decade many teachers had begun working with each other on courses of study and modes of assessment appropriate to their students. They learnt to call on the support of their professional associations, local advisory bodies, local teachers' centres, the Schools Council and other national research or curriculum groups. In short, in response to new demands, teachers undertook forms of in-service education which changed the level of their classroom transactions. While many of these developments subserved the examination system, they represented a general transition to the 'second level', at which teachers' responsibility for what they teach ceases to be nominal and becomes a matter of serious planning and testing. Although not widely appreciated outside, this transition is now largely taken for granted in the schools themselves. Not all teachers take a positive role in O level or CSE work, but those who have committed themselves to teacher-controlled examining at 16 plus have effected such developments in the construction of curricula and in modes of assessment as to bridge the traditional gap between the functions of teaching and examining.

Despite the constraints imposed by the examination system and the lack of definition of the general revolution affecting secondary classrooms as the bulk of teachers are drawn into work at level two, some heads and teachers have taken deliberate steps towards the third level of educational transaction. At this level, students are positively involved with their teachers in planning, recording and assessing their individual purposes, programmes and progress. In some schools, these efforts are associated with particular groups of students only, or with special subject areas in the hands of certain teachers. However limited at present, such efforts point the way to the possibility of a more general advance towards level three. At this level the relationship of the student and the teacher is one of mutual respect with each trying to enable the youngster to make something of his own life. Perhaps this has always been the aim: but in many schools neither the student nor the teacher acts as though it were.

Most teachers are themselves the product of a prolonged tutelage system of success in examination hurdles. Many of them reach the teacher's side of the desk without having given more than cursory consideration to the skills and qualities – as distinct from the subject knowledge – needed by the teacher in the classroom. They may have attended many lectures but have had little experience of listening to their peers, still less of seeking out the meaning in what children at school try to say. Teachers have usually shown themselves able to compete in the educational stakes but to have little training in group work or in finding clues to meaning in non-verbal forms of communication. As suggested above, the transition to level two has been achieved mainly by school-based in-service education related to the development of the CSE. That to level three, on the other hand, can be ascribed largely to the influence of individual heads and teachers, notably those concerned with non-examined pupils. However ill-prepared for their task, some teachers try to deal positively with boys and girls who expect to leave secondary school without entering for any examination. It could well be that some of the work that has gone into attempts to increase the competencies and to build the self-esteem of non-examined pupils has relevance for all boys and girls of the age group. The division into examined and non-examined at the age of 16 is not required in law nor supportable within the principle of comprehensive education as secondary schools up and down the country try to interpret it. It now behoves educators everywhere to look closely not only at school examinations – which has been done already ad nauseam – but at positive efforts to cater educationally for the non-examined group and to explore alternatives to examinations for the examined group.

There is some justice in the claim of many schools to have advanced as far as possible within the limits set by their human and financial resources and by the national system of 16 plus examinations. Their claims are borne out by a group of Her Majesty's Inspectors. A recent publication gives their comments on ten good secondary schools. They considered the chosen schools to be successful in achieving a match between the ability and aptitudes of their pupils and the academic and social standards they attained. Various other dimensions of quality were described, among them good relationships, with mutual respect obtaining between adults and pupils. The HMIs were greatly impressed by the amount of deliberate planning undertaken by successful schools. They concluded: 'The schools see themselves as places designed for learning; they take trouble to make their philosophies explicit for themselves and to explain them to parents and pupils; the foundation of their work and corporate life is an acceptance of shared values. Emphasis is laid on consultation, team work and participation, but without exception, the most important single factor in the success of these schools is the quality of leadership of the head . . .'

The HMIs' paper puts the accolade of approval on school-based in-service education. It shows that the credit for providing appropriately for students of compulsory school age lies with those heads and teachers who get to grips continually with the formidable responsibilities devolving on them under the Education Act. They claim that the characteristics which they applaud might be emulated by any school.

So much for the general progress that has been made nationally. Part II of this book is in effect a series of case studies of progress made in individual areas, by teachers and researchers, in developing practical expressions of the third level of relationship between student and teacher. The school-based initiatives recorded here are the best-documented examples of their kind. They mark the end of the period in which the educational service can be satisfied to drain its resources into an examination system of limited value, while denying any recognition or support for teachers or their organisations endeavouring to meet the needs of their pupils in the total circumstances of the present day; endeavouring, moreover, to develop practical means by which their accountability can be shown. As the Scottish head teachers wrote at the end of the section on the aims of their working party: 'As headteachers, we wish to make it clear that parents and others are at least getting their money's worth. We are worried about the rumour of falling standards, declining literacy, university misfits. Are they true? How do we know? We are worried about the much-advertised malaise in the teaching profession, uncertain about what we are supposed to do, about our objectives. Many of us find that recently the range of skills required of the teacher have been diminished. The implementation of the procedures outlined in this report might do much towards our self-respect, our authority and our image.'

The time for pious hopes is past. What is urgent now is for official recognition of the key role of school-based initiatives and of school-based in-service education of teachers. Now, a nationally sponsored effort could clarify the principles and practices of third level transactions in school; and it could establish the machinery, including the validating procedures whereby 16 year olds could begin soon to claim positive evidence in the form of statements concerning their educational stature and general characteristics. The third part of this book proposes a new system of statements for 16 year olds, nationally validated, which offers one way in which this can be done.

Part II
Progress Towards a Solution

2 English at Comberton Village College

JOHN BLANCHARD

A file for each pupil

The first part of this chapter describes how English teachers in an 11 to 16 comprehensive school devised a scheme of assessment which includes statements by pupils about their work.[1]

In the not very distant past, there was an English Department in a rural, mixed, two- or three-form entry secondary modern school, whose teachers taught to an implicitly agreed general syllabus, devoting much individual attention to pupils who at 16 sat GCE or CSE, or left without certificated qualification. By 1974 the established order had been shaken. The school was developing as a comprehensive in an increasingly populated area; two years were already of six-form entry, and a third year of comprehensive intake, a 'bulge' year seven-form entry, was about to be welcomed. The teachers no longer 'knew' all of the pupils and could no longer feel confident that they were meeting the pupils' needs in the early years or guiding the pupils towards appropriate public examinations in their final year.

During the past three years the teachers have come to discomforting realisations about organisational inadequacies and chose to act on them in a piecemeal, pragmatic way, with the result that a scheme has gradually been constructed, already tried in a number of respects, and will be operating fully from September 1978. Our initial need was to agree principles and practices of monitoring pupils' progress and of grouping pupils most advantageously. The scheme began as a means of improving administrative arrangements, has consequently affected methods of assessment, and now provides the basis on which to develop teaching method in the future.

Our first step was to adopt one of the recommendations made in the Bullock Committee's Report, *A Language For Life*. One teacher took responsibility for monitoring the progress in reading and writing of our Lower School pupils, so that we could identify those who need supportive

[1] I am indebted to many colleagues and friends for their collaboration and inspiration in the devising of the scheme, and especially to Alison Littlefair and Jae Milgate.

teaching. The teacher opened a file for each of our first and second year pupils in order to collect their standardised Reading Age tests and examples of their writing completed twice in each of those years. At the same time we were designing, together with Primary School colleagues in the catchment area, a format for records which would extend our picture of pupils' language development. There is now for each of the entrants to our first year a record from the local Primary Schools which states:
– the latest Reading Age score, the date and name of the test;
– the name of Language Workshops used, and the level reached;
– a reading record for the Spring Term of the final Primary year;
– a piece of dated, unmarked, creative writing.

We had, then, begun to document individual pupils' progress. We next saw the need to monitor and exchange information between ourselves about our teaching of classes. We draw up a practical syllabus in the shape of a relatively exhaustive checklist of activities and skills, under four headings: Talking, Listening, Writing and Reading. There are, for example, items under the first heading such as:
– group discussion in the absence of teacher;
– group discussion in the presence of teacher;
– pupil panel addressing the class;
– class discussion chaired by the teacher.

While the checklist keeps open the teachers' options to adopt, for example, a 'thematic' approach, a 'class reader' approach, a skill or concept based approach, or a course book approach, the teachers' attention is drawn to activities, skills and concepts of fundamental value. More specifically, some items in the list are prefaced by a year group number which prescribes the teaching of certain things at some time during the course of certain secondary years. And, since the checklists for every class are passed to the Head of Department at the end of each year, they serve both prospective and retrospective functions.

Our school has a policy of annual examinations, grades and reports. We decided to implement that policy quite rigorously and to apply it to our use of the checklist and the pupils' files. We composed examination papers so that they test the skills which we were proposing should be exercised by pupils in specific year groups. The first year pupils' examination, for example, includes invitations to writing of an informal kind addressed to a real or imaginary, but definite, audience, and to writing about books. The pupils' scripts, we thought, could be usefully stored in the files, together with copies of the annual report to parents. We decided to base report grades on performance in school examinations.

Each of the Lower School pupils' tests is now graded 'across the year' on a curve of equal distribution: C being the median grade, and there being as many Bs as Ds, as many As as Es. The test grades are totalled and averaged, yielding for each pupil a norm-referenced, test-based grade, which the class teacher may finally moderate, for the purpose of the school report to parents, by one third of a grade in the light of the pupil's work during the year. Thus, test grade C might become C+ or C−, if the teacher considers progress or effort or attainment warrants such up- or downgrading.

The process appears impersonal and coldly calculated perhaps, but it was, after all, our intention to record and file periodic, formal assessments of pupils' progress. The result, as far as the parents are concerned, is the kind of report which is instantly recognisable as the teachers' normal assessment. As far as the pupils are concerned, it provides the kind of 'hard facts' assessment to which they become accustomed in most secondary school subjects; for example, as follows:

Carol reads well and writes accurately. She is a helpful and pleasant member of the class. A good year's work.
Grade: B

Tom finds reading difficult. His writing is sometimes interesting, but is poorly presented, lacking correct spelling, punctuation, and so on.
He tries hard.
Grade: D

Such reports and grades might help to answer parents' questions about how well their children are doing, but they do not necessarily encourage the pupils to view their work as something they develop. Having agreed in the Lower School a distinct procedure and context for grades and statements of summative assessment, in the reports to parents and in the files, it became possible for us to consider viewing pupils' day-to-day work in a far less judgemental way, measuring pupils neither against one another, nor against supposedly objective standards of excellence. We realised that we do not have to grade, quantify or qualify pupils' daily work; we can rather take a descriptive, constructive view, making a responsive, positive assessment of their unique endeavours, talents and needs. At this point we sought a different tone for current or continuous assessment: a means of addressing the pupils in a formal, yet personal way in order to focus on their individual development. In order to establish that tone, so that it would be distinguishable for teachers and pupils alike, a quite separate channel of communication was suggested.

A system of reports to pupils was proposed, to allow for such a style of formative assessment by the teachers. These reports are for the pupils, kept by them and so not included in the files, and are written at times when pupils may be expected to be reviewing their past work and looking to the future: at the end of the first year, after the first term of the second year, and at the beginning and end of the third year.

For Lower School pupils, then, teachers write under the headings Reading, Writing, Talking and Listening and Homework; for example, as follows:

To Carol Lambert 1L from Mr Blanchard   Date . . . . .
Reading: You have understood and enjoyed books by Joan Tate, E. Nesbit and others. I can recommend Nina Bawden, Rosemary Sutcliff and Alan Garner.
Writing: Your neat and careful descriptions are pleasing to read. I wonder if you can think of ways to include moods and feelings in your writing. Try to write in funny, sad, eerie, and other ways, if you can.
Talking and Listening: Your report on television programmes showed careful planning. You have asked helpful questions about your friends' reports as well. Sometimes I think you speak so quietly that others cannot hear you.
Homework: I am pleased that you read at home, quite apart from what is set. Do you ever do projects in your spare time?

The distinction between the two kinds of assessment is worth emphasising. On the one hand, summative assessment defines the quality of pupils' work at any given time, is conveniently expressed in terms of a grade or score, and may be found useful by people other than the teachers and pupils, such as parents, employers, teachers in other schools and in Further Education. Formative assessment, on the other hand, is an aid to teaching and learning; it takes account of work at present by looking back over the past, in order to look forward to future development; it is ideally expressed in terms of a statement, and may not be found useful by people other than those directly involved in the learning process. Both are proper forms of assessment, in that they take stock of the results of learning; but summative assessment tends to freeze time, to isolate performance and competence from their developmental context and, because it can be imagined to deal in absolute, objective values, lends itself to being thought of as a means of conclusively classifying people.

It became clear that the scheme for the Lower School could not apply in identical fashion to the Upper School. While norm-referenced grading can apply in the Lower School from 11 to 13, the Upper School courses from 14 to 16 seem to call for criterion-referenced grading, based on what we understand to be the standards of Public Examination Boards. For Upper School pupils, furthermore, it is not so easy to separate summative from formative assessments, perhaps because, as Public Examinations approach, learning seems to become more a matter of gaining qualifications, and less a matter of developing oneself. The implied element of 'continuous' assessment for CSE also makes it difficult for teachers to address pupils, as they may on occasions in the Lower School, in a non-grading, non-judgemental way.

These considerations led us to introduce in the Upper School a practice of making both summative, graded assessment and formative, personal assessment, at the end of each half-term. We defined the grades literally in relation to those of our Public Examination Boards. Thus, A, B and C represent GCE pass standard grades; C also represents CSE grade 1 standard; C−, D+, D, D− and E represent CSE grades 2, 3, 4, 5 and ungraded Public Examination standard respectively. The statements, written in the pupils' folders of writing, refer, then, to competence in relation to the standards by which pupils are ultimately measured in Public Examinations at 16, to effort and performance in relation to the individual pupil's capacity (for which an individual 'effort grade' is awarded, C indicating a satisfactory minimum of work by what we understand to be the pupil's own standards), and to progress which pupils might make in the future; for example, as follows:

Tony
Your war stories are well planned and action-packed, and they will gain you credit as part of your CSE course work. More types of writing will gain you more credit. Why not write about stories you have read and films you have seen? You could also write about war in a factual way or in a documentary style, for example, from the point of view of someone affected by war. I can help you with reference books. If you find you are not getting on very well with a piece of work, why not talk to me about it? You can change work to suit yourself. Wouldn't that be better than just leaving it?
Grade for Language and Literature: D.   *Grade for Effort: C+.*
                                          JB   Date . . . . .

Parents of Upper School pupils continue to receive their reports in much the same way as parents of Lower School pupils, except that the grades indicate how pupils stand in relation to Public Examinations' standards. Copies of those reports go to the files, together with school examination scripts. As a result, by the time pupils are in the Upper School, the files have the clear character of records providing a chronological catalogue of summative assessments. Statements of formative assessment by teachers are excluded from the files because we wish to make it quite clear to the pupils that such statements are intended to guide them in their future learning rather than to judge them.

Having taken measures which seek to ensure certain kinds of response on the part of the pupils to our assessments, it was only appropriate that we should consider their response in an active sense, rather than passively as we had so far done. Customarily, pupils have little or no opportunity to respond to assessment. We realised that pupils can both respond to and contribute towards assessment. The pupils, we decided, should have access to their files and make statements of self-assessment, to be kept in the files. Suitable times for pupils' writing such statements are towards the end of their first and second years, early and late in their third and fourth years, and on three occasions in their fifth year. Teachers may discuss the pupils' statements with them, if the pupils so wish, but may not direct their writing. Pupils are encouraged to write about their interests, their pleasures and frustrations, ambitions and doubts in the subject. It is for them to write as they choose, knowing that what they write may affect the teaching they receive; for example, as follows:

> *To Mr Blanchard*   *Date . . .*
> *I don't like it when we all have to read the same book together. I can't keep up sometimes and sometimes I want to carry on when we have to stop. I want to do more writing to make it neater. I like discussing problems but sometimes people just mess about.*
>
> *Tim Barrow 2S*

The pupils' statements are a bridge between summative and formative assessments. They are themselves an assessment of the two kinds: stating and demonstrating competence at a given time; and giving teachers clues about how to facilitate further learning.

Very significantly, the pupils can learn from the scheme that assessment does not have to be a word or letter or score which eternally damns or saves. They can see in their files how assessments accumulate and change as their work accumulates and changes. They can see that they have an important part to play in assessment. They can see that we all periodically take stock in order to decide future courses of action.

The pupils' final statement inevitably performs this function, since it allows pupils to review their experience of the subject over the whole period of secondary schooling. The statement at 16 provides pupils with an ideal opportunity to address themselves to questions which they feel prospective employers or Further Education teachers would like to have answered; for example, as follows:

> *To whom it may concern: A statement about my English work*
> *Although I have quite enjoyed reading novels, plays and poems in English, I really like to read factual books. My hobbies are collecting bottles, mending things and going for walks. I will always read a book about any of those things if I find one. I usually read the newspaper or part of it.*
> *I liked doing projects on my hobbies, especially on horses when I was horse mad. I never really got interested in writing stories. But I did like it when we wrote sort of poems about ourselves and other people.*
> *I want to work in a shop or an office and I think I can manage instructions in writing, writing letters and keeping records. My teachers and my mother say I am*

a tidy-minded person. My exam results won't be very special, but I have been trying to work for a CSE grade three.

My folder shows all of my writing from the last two years. I choose the script and essay on the different ways different people talk and behave in shops as my best work. I wrote about managers, senior, junior and part-time assistants and of course most important of all – the customers. And I made a tape of the script.

R. Darlow   Date . . . . .

Having decided to include pupils' statements as part of our assessment and to keep them in the files, it was a small step to the proposition that pupils could and should design, pursue and assess their own programmes of work. There might have been a danger that pupils would not respond to the invitation to write statements of self-assessment and self-orientation, if they had not the opportunity to work under their own instructions rather than the teachers'. So it is proposed that, before pupils write their statements for the files, they should undertake their own course of learning.

There are two constraints on this independent work: unavoidable limitations on resources, and the requirement that the pupils first write an introduction, as below, and, after the teacher has read it, that they write a plan for their work. This introduction was completed by a 14 year old boy:

1   There are four main language activities:
    Talking, Listening, Reading and Writing,
    which may be connected with the activity of Making Things.
    I wish to concentrate on *Reading*.

2   Complete one or more of these:
    I wish to present . . . . .
    I wish to produce . . . . .
    I wish to study *Science Fiction*.
    I wish to improve . . . . .
    I wish to read *Science Fiction stories*.
    I wish to write . . . . .
    I wish to . . . . .

3   The help I will need is *to be shown Science Fiction books to read*.

Robert King   3F   Date . . . . .

Such work encourages the teacher to perform the role of supportive, enabling assistant and the pupils to perform the role of self-directing agent. The teachers can help the pupils assess their work, but the rewards and disappointments are the pupils' because the work really is their own.

Three or four years ago, then, we started with the intention of monitoring individual pupils' progress. Now we have a scheme which

attempts to take account of many forms of assessment: by school and public examination, by personal and parents' reports, by grades and statements, by pupils and teachers. We can summarise the main elements of the whole scheme, as follows:
– a practical syllabus (checklist of activities and skills);
– teachers' reports to pupils;
– pupils' own programmes of work;
– pupils' files, which contain:
  – a Primary School record;
  – Reading Age tests;
  – school examination scripts, with grades, and other examples of pupils' work;
  – copies of reports to parents;
  – pupils' statements.
It is the file, its contents, purpose and implications, which are the focus for the second part of this chapter.

Contents, purpose and implications

Right away, I should like to draw out two important implications. One is that it seems necessary to persist with some existing assessment procedures until significant changes are agreed by everyone concerned with 16 year olds, and that teachers may prompt progress by separating the different elements and results of different styles of assessment.

I am suggesting that, for the present, school records be one kind of assessment, and Public Examination grades be another kind, which may develop in the future the same validating procedure, and that the school and pupils provide access to whichever interested parties may request. In practice, varied kinds of assessment are sought, ranging, for example, from general character reference to specific academic record, from judgement of pupils' self-awareness and self-motivation to their knowledge of particular skills and items of information. Until there is developed a form of documentation which meets the widely varying needs of those who select 16 year olds for employment and study, there would seem to be much in favour of maintaining separable kinds of assessment.

A second implication is, I think, that the scheme, described in this chapter and developed by one department, can apply to all secondary school departments. There should be no reason to think that what is suggested can apply only to the subject of English.

For everyone concerned with 16 year olds answers to three main questions are sought:
(a) What do pupils do at school?

(b) How good are they at it?

(c) How does pupils' school work relate to what they may do after the age of 16?

In some ways it is easier to answer the question: How are pupils usually assessed up to and at the age of 16? In answering this question we can locate three main kinds of assessment:

(i) In the ordinary course of events, pupils perform tasks which are corrected, marked or graded by teachers, without there necessarily being any common standards or approach amongst teachers.

(ii) Periodically, pupils' work is assessed by teachers in reports to parents; these may be norm-referenced or criterion-referenced; different teachers may apply uniform or diverse standards; and parents and pupils may be ignorant of whatever principles govern assessment.

(iii) At 16, pupils' competence may be assessed by Public Examination Boards, operating a variety of principles and practices, none of which may be clear to anyone who views the final grades.

We can ask: What is the connection between the questions (a), (b) and (c) and the customary methods of assessment (i), (ii) and (iii) above?

Clearly, (i) relates to (a): pupils work in school and their work is assessed by teachers. Conventionally, only pupils and teachers view such performance and assessment.

Further, (ii) relates to (b): teachers judge pupils' competence and make statements to parents about it. Conventionally, parents receive them and pupils read them.

Finally, (iii) relates to (c): examination boards judge the candidates' competence and issue grades by way of assessment. Conventionally, the teachers and pupils receive them and any interested body may ask to view the assessment, but its notation and meaning may be indecipherable if the examinations, their syllabuses, values and assessment priorities are not understood.

Pupils who do not sit Public Examinations, then, are subject only to limited, idiosyncratic assessment by teachers. It is worth noting the two faults in the present system: both the closed and idiosyncratic nature of school assessment, and the exclusion of some pupils from a comprehensive, public form of assessment. Teachers have tried to remedy one or other of the faults in their own ways. Some (including Don Stansbury, for example) have developed schemes principally for 'non-examination' pupils. Others (including the designers of this scheme and contributors towards CSE and GCE syllabuses, for example) have initially accepted that a number of pupils 'fail' to enter for Public Examinations, and looked towards improving statements of assessment for pupils who are examination candidates. Significantly, whether one sets out with the 'unacademic' or the 'academic' pupils in mind, one promptly arrives at a point where existing school record systems and Public Examinations appear unsatisfactory.

Perhaps the most startling oversight on the part of teachers and examiners is their failure to take note of the very people who are their concern: the pupils. The existing patterns of assessment, locally idiosyncratic and public alike, neglect the pupils' capacity to document and assess their own performance and competence. The present system excludes self-assessment: no pupil, however 'academic' or skilled, is trusted to take public account of her/his interests, experience, strengths and weaknesses.

Let us return to three major questions, (a), (b) and (c). How might answers to those questions be supplied and made accessible to interested bodies, such as employers and Further Education teachers? The answer here proposed is that the Secondary School should document pupils' progress and include both teachers' records and pupils' statements of self-assessment as indispensable elements of the documentation.

The inclusion of pupils' statements must be stressed. If employers and tutors are realistically to assess applicants' prospects, they cannot rely solely, or even predominantly, on the judgements of third parties, that is, of teachers and examiners. Young adults' self-orientation is crucial after the age of 16: they have to seek employment or study which will suit them. This scheme proposes to make pupils' self-orientation crucial to their learning at school as well.

At the centre of the scheme is a file for each pupil, maintained by teachers, and open to pupils and their parents. The file contains:
– 'objective' tests, undertaken once or twice a year;
– examples of pupils' work, assessed by teachers;
– copies of public statements of assessment by teachers, for example, to parents;
– statements of self-assessment by pupils.
The file is accessible to any interested body, at the teachers' and pupils' discretion. The file collects and opens to view:
   (a) what pupils do at school;
   (b) how good pupils are at their work;
and the pupils' statements at 16, separable from the file, allow them
   (c) to describe and demonstrate their experience of and aptitude for tasks which they perceive as relevant to their future occupations.

It is important that pupils may study their files whenever they come to write their statements. And the final statements, written at 16, review their Secondary School experience and look forward to what might follow. The scheme allows pupils, therefore, to address themselves to the vital question (c) and relate their past performance and present competence to the demands of their future careers.

Such a scheme might promote a revision of public examinations, inasmuch as a file containing a valid cross-section of pupils' work during their final two years of Secondary School might be the most appropriate object of professional assessment. An extension of the Joint Matriculation Board's combined GCE/CSE examinations at 16 plus might admirably suit this scheme's requirement that files contain 'objective' tests and examples of pupils' work, as well as pupils' statements.

In the particular case of English, pupils might present between the ages of 14 and 16 examples of:
- standardised Reading Age tests;
- comprehension exercises in the form of answers to 'closed' questions;
- comprehension exercises in the form of 'open' response to textual stimulus;
- writing of different kinds – informal, expressive;
  - informal, informative;
  - formal, instructive, discursive and persuasive;
  - creative, narrative, verse or dramatic.

A similar approach would seem to be applicable in other school subjects. Pupils might be required to demonstrate their understanding of and response to material and ideas, and to demonstrate their own development of material and ideas with reference to agreed subject matter and disciplines. Offering a limited sample of work which meets minimum specifications and allows for pupils' initiative in the choice of additional work might become an approved approach to the problem of what pupils are to do in order that their competence may be assessed.

Such an approach might dispel the confusion and divisiveness which now exist between CSE and GCE. It would allow documentation and authoritative, validated assessment of pupils' work under a modified system of Examinations Boards.

But it must be recognised that such an approach does not in itself answer the major criticisms of the present arrangements for assessment at 16, summarised in Part I of this book. Unless the pupils address themselves to the question of assessment, solutions to the central problems remain inadequate, however neat they may seem. Assessment simply cannot be the prerogative of the educators.

It is for that reason that the pupils' statements of self-assessment provide the cornerstone of the scheme. The scheme is designed to benefit everyone associated with the results of secondary schooling.

The scheme benefits interested bodies outside the schools. Teachers are well placed to answer the question about how good pupils are at their work, but employers and teachers in Further Education can learn at least as much, about what pupils actually do and how their work relates to careers after 16, directly from the pupils. Under this scheme, the school's files contain all three as distinct elements.

The scheme benefits teachers. While teachers alone assess secondary school pupils' performance up to the point of public examination, they are frustrated in their other role (of teaching) by the unilateral nature of the enterprise. If instruction and assessment by teachers were the sole pre-requisites for learning, there would be no need for pupils to assess themselves. But teachers know that learning involves self-appraisal. Learning and teaching are not only enhanced by the learners' self-orientation, self-motivation and self-awareness; they only become real, meaningful and effective as the learners develop and exercise those capacities.

The scheme benefits pupils. Pupils' learning is stimulated by their knowing what they can do and what they cannot do, and by their knowing what they would like to do. They need to be able to represent what they know to themselves, and might most usefully combine the opportunity so to do with the opportunity to address a wider audience, stating what they know for the benefit of others who may wish to know the same.

If pupils are to be aware of their capacities and achievements, they must have the opportunity to formulate such awareness. This the scheme proposes in the file.

If pupils are to formulate their awareness of interest, competence, need and ambition, they must have the opportunity to act on them themselves. This the scheme proposes. Periodically, and at least for a time before they write their statements for the files, pupils design, pursue and assess their own programmes of work.

Conventionally, teachers already encourage pupils to 'do projects', perhaps once a year. At such times, pupils choose their own area of interest and present work much as they choose. But this practice often appears to have nothing to do with 'real work' ('real' by the teachers' definition), because the teachers' and ultimately the examiners' assessment may take no account of it: the pupils produce the work to little public purpose, knowing that, however they may view it themselves, self-assessment has no recognised value. The scheme suggests that teachers support the pupils in their choice of activities, aims and materials, so encouraging two forms of self-assessment in the pupils: during the course of the work the pupils judge their progress in order to decide further development; and at the end of the programme the pupils are in a position to make a statement for the file, and so for others, who might be interested in their performance, competence and view of themselves.

If pupils are to view learning as anything other than the more or less successful expression of what they have been taught, they must have the opportunity to see their teachers as teachers, engaged with them in the experience of learning, rather than predominantly as assessors. This the scheme proposes by locating teachers' summative assessment firmly in the context of the file, so that teachers' formative assessment be allowed to play its vital part in the context of the teaching and learning process.

The scheme comprises three elements then: at a public or national level, professional, standardised or 'objective' examiners' assessment; at a local level, the school teachers' assessment; and, at an individual level, the pupils' statements. The three elements are separable, but contained as a file.

There can be no reason why the different levels should imply different degrees of acceptability or validity, why, for example, pupils' or teachers' assessments should by nature or definition be less valid than public examiners' assessments. Teachers have already demonstrated, by their administration of CSE and participation in GCE management, that their assessment is valid provided proper procedures exist. Pupils demonstrate, by their eagerness and ability to make as full and appropriate applications to employment and study at 16 as any applicants to any other posts, that they may provide self-assessment which is valid provided proper procedures exist.

All three elements, then, might be validated by a national Board, locally or regionally organised, operating in much the same way as CSE Mode III Boards now function, whose task it would be to ensure standardisation and appropriateness in assessment and selection at 16.

Such Boards at national and local levels would most profitably include representatives from employment, from Secondary School management and teaching staff, from the community, and from Further Education.

The most important test of the different assessments' validity, however, is their usefulness and relevance to the users, namely the employers and Further Education teachers who welcome young adults at 16. At present the professional examiners' assessment is proving far less useful and relevant to the users than is desired.

3 Evaluation and learning in secondary schools

JACK WHITEHEAD AND JOAN WHITEHEAD

'*Surely there must be a way to obtain an objective record of a pupil's progress and the effect that a course of study is having on him. It should be possible to build up a profile of each pupil in situ. It should be so designed that a glance will reveal a valuable and, as far as possible, objective profile of the pupil.*'[1]

Teachers will be familiar with these problems of relating evaluation to learning and of ensuring objectivity in assessment. The latter in particular has been a source of tension between advocates of CSE Mode I and of O level examinations upheld as 'objective' indices of attainment, and supporters of CSE Mode III assessment, not infrequently demeaned as 'subjective'.

The purpose of this chapter is to suggest a form of student profile, which is 'subjective' in detailing the student's own personal development and attainment, but which would be 'objective' by virtue of being nationally validated and subjected to moderation procedures similar to those in Mode III. As this profile was built up, it would help the teacher to determine the course of learning for each student: it would be diagnostic of present achievement and indicative of the next stage of learning. On completion, it would help to place the student in employment or higher education. In other words, it would continue to fulfil the selective function played by the present system of examinations, yet would do so in a way which enabled evaluation to arise from learning and would provide a diagnostic record of each student. Its selective potential, moreover, would be extended to include a detailed summary of a broad spectrum of an individual's skills, aptitudes and abilities – arguably a finer instrument to predict an employee's, trainee's or undergraduate's future potential.

Before providing two examples of profiles at present applied in school science departments, some assumptions, limitations and possibilities of the present system of evaluation in O level and Modes I and II and III examinations will be discussed.

Assumptions, limitations and possibilities of current examinations

A central issue in the debate about evaluation and examinations concerns the objectivity and validity of the results. The view accepted by selectors for jobs and higher education is that the procedures employed at present by O level boards can be trusted to give 'objective' and 'valid' statements about students' learning and about their performance relative to other students. The criterion of validity used in O levels is known as content validity: it assumes a given body of knowledge and requires candidates to display their mastery of the content. The objectivity of the examination is conferred by a statistical analysis of the items of the tests and the ordering of the results into a grading system. In this grading, success is defined by reference to 20 per cent of the age group (the results, in other words, are 'norm referenced'). What this form of examining omits, however, is any evaluation of the pupils' own enquiries into the meaning of the subject: in science it omits any evaluation of the student's questions, ideas, problems and hypotheses. This omission of construct validity is a major limitation of Mode I examinations, and hence such examinations should be treated more cautiously by selectors as an indicator of a student's ability to do the subject.

It is with an awareness of such limitations that some teachers have attempted to implement Mode III examinations with 100 per cent coursework assessment.[2] Here the student's own constructs and meanings throughout their course can also be monitored and evaluated. This offers a more accurate assessment of the student's overall competence in a subject and influences what happens in the classroom. The teacher can structure progressively the most relevant learning experiences for students depending on each individual's development. The difficulty is that while such an assessment scheme may be acceptable in preventing a divorce between evaluation and learning, it may also appear to forfeit any claim to objectivity. It is both individualised and depends on teachers' subjective assessments of student performance.

To counteract such charges, rigorous internal and external moderation procedures have been established in which teachers' assessments of students' work are subjected to the criticisms of other teachers and external moderators. In other words, objectivity is not conferred, as in Mode I, through statistical analysis: it is derived through mutual control and criticism. This kind of scheme can therefore meet the demands of objectivity and validity and could provide a basis for a nationally validated system of statements for 16 year olds.

Two examples of the integration of evaluation and learning

This will be clear from two examples of the actual system of evaluation underpinning this proposal. Both are from schemes devised by groups of science teachers working with the 11 to 14 age group but embody features which could be incorporated into profiles for the 14 to 16 age group.

It is not from any lack of commitment on the part of the teachers that these schemes have not been so extended. Rather it is indicative of the political climate and a fear of jeopardising their students' life-chances by using testing procedures outside the traditional examination system. In both examples the teachers were concerned to relate their evaluation procedures to pupils' learning, that is, to chart each child's unique developmental sequence as well as recording a terminal assessment. Since one of their fundamental assumptions was a recognition of the differences between students' abilities and interests, they recognised that the same concepts could be grasped by students through a variety of approaches. In response to these differences the teachers sought to offer students more choice in their learning and responsibility for it. Thus this account contains details of the conditions of learning from which the student profiles were constructed.

Example A

This approach was developed by science teachers with the assistance of the Avon Resources for Learning Unit,[3] a body established in 1974 to investigate the claims of advocates of resource-based learning. The pattern of learning involves students in study tours beginning and ending with a consultation between teacher and pupil. From this consultation the student is usually directed to a set of task cards in which instructions are given on the use of resources and equipment. When none of the task cards is able to meet the needs of the student the teacher devises a unique activity for the student or makes alterations to an existing task card. At the simplest level, the relationship between the components of the system can be represented in the diagram on p. 33.

The teacher monitors each student's progress through the task cards with the aid of record cards of the type on p. 34. This card was designed for the topic electricity, and it contains statements of the student's progress and achievements. It reveals at a glance the tasks completed, the results of homework and tests, and the teacher's comments.

However, the statements given are mainly on the subject content. They do not meet the additional requirements for construct validity and consideration of other qualities (presentation, effect, written communication and research originality) delineated in the example B below.

Example B

This approach was developed by two teachers, Maggie Hannon and

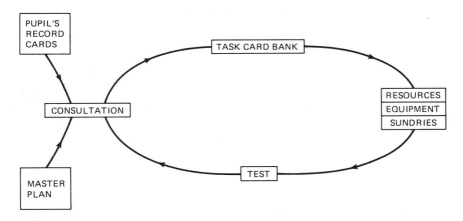

Tony Cole, of the Schools Council Mixed Ability Project.[4] These teachers moved over a period of three years from class teaching in mixed ability groups to an approach where students could study different topics using independent enquiry learning methods. They put together a scheme of topics in such a way that children could 'find their way through a particular topic, and also answer questions posed by themselves in these topics which may not actually be part of the subject material'.[5] They were concerned to offer possibilities for the exercise of students' initiative which was not found in Example A.

Needing an effective method of monitoring their students' progress, as indicated in the introductory remark of this chapter, they developed the system reported below in the form it is given to the staff in the science department where it is being used.

Profile assessment for mixed ability groups in combined science[6]

Aims
1) To achieve a standardised profile of pupils' progress through topics:
   (a) in the academic sense
   (b) in the way they approach and present their work.
2) To enable teacher, parent and child to monitor changes in achievement, attitude and effort (from records at the time) of deliberate stages in the learning process.

Areas of assessment and scores
The areas finally decided as being most useful were as follows:
A   Presentation
B   Effort
C   Written communication
D   Research

NAME: JANET HODGES   CLASS: 2Q   ELECTRICITY

Topic	
USE OF CIRCUIT BOARD	✓
SERIES & PARALLEL CIRCUITS	✓
CIRCUIT DESIGN	✓
AMMETER	✓
HEATING & FUSES	
WIRING A PLUG	
CONDUCTORS & INSULATORS	
ELECTRO-MAGNETS	
MAGNETISM	
CELLS AND BATTERIES	
VOLTAGE	
DIMMERS & RECTIFIERS	

DATE	TASK	COMMENTS
12/1/78	2, 3	✓ Use correct circuit symbols. Good knowledge of house wiring circuits.
16/1/78	7 →	Try building your circuit on a circuit board. Use bell in Tray 9
19/1/78	8	v. good idea.
23/1/78	11	Discuss scale readings.
26/1/78	14	Excellent writing on new use of elect. Well done.
"	Test 1	
30/1/78	21 →	Also wire up the light socket (tray 6)

HOMEWORK

1	7	6
2	5	7
3	8	8
4		9
5		10

TESTS

1	8
2	
3	
Final Asses.	

HODGES Janet	1	2	3	4	5	6	7	8	9	10	11	12	13	14	15	16	17	18	19	20	21	22	23	24	25	26	27	28	29	30	31	32	33	34	35	36	37	38	39	40

E   A standardised 'core' test

Areas A–D are marked on a scale from one to four – one being the highest score possible. These numbers were chosen deliberately so that there is no 'average' score.

Detailed breakdown of scores

A   *Presentation*

  1   Neat writing. Includes lots of good diagrams.
  2   Reasonable writing. Adequate number of reasonable diagrams.
  3   Poor writing. Shoddy but recognisable diagrams.
  4   Writing illegible or nearly so. Few diagrams of very poor appearance.

B   *Effort* (This to be related directly to child and not necessarily to the standard of work of results. Thus the less able might score high in effort.)

  1   A constant maximum 'trier' in the topic.
  2   Consistently tries hard, needing only occasional encouragement.
  3   The inconsistent approach – constant 'prodding' at certain times allied to keenness at others.
  4   An unsettled and lazy approach needing *constant* prodding.

C   *Communication*

  1   Written work consistently explains the achievements sensibly and in good English.
  2   Written work often explains the achievements sensibly and in good English.
  3   Written work sometimes explains the achievements sensibly and in good English.
  4   Written work is disjointed, making little sense.

D   *Research* (Again a quality not necessarily shown by the high achiever.)

  1   Regularly shows originality of thought or action beyond that taught or set.
  2   Now and again shows qualities as in 1.
  3   Rarely shows qualities as in 1.
  4   For their ability they are doing as required, yet have shown no originality or initiative in the topic. (This person could still be top of the class in other respects.)

Frequency of assessment

Written assessment is to be made at the end of each topic, at the time the core test is given (although it is desirable that the four more subjective assessments are decided before the test mark is known!)

Several interim assessments should be communicated to the students during the topic via teachers' comments in the exercise books – the number depending on the length of the topic.

It would be possible for a variability score to be shown for students who change markedly during a topic e.g.

EFFORT 3–1

Method of recording assessments

This is to be incorporated in the topic title page at the beginning of the topic – the actual layout to be communicated to students and staff on a separate sheet.

There will be space on the page for comments as well as scores – such things as students' continuity of work through the topic, attitude to homework and constructive criticism should be included here.

Subject assessments are shown as scores from 1–4, whereas the test results will be shown as a mark against the maximum for that test, e.g. 27/50.

Comments

Effort	
Presentation	
Communication	
Research	
Test	

Topic	
Name	
House Group	
Date	

Practical issues of implementation

Neither of these examples should be seen as a blueprint for action. They are offered to stimulate debate about which particular abilities, skills and qualities should be incorporated into profiles for 16 year olds. The emphasis on these various attributes will, moreover, be dependent on the particular subject under discussion. For example, a student's profile in modern languages will necessarily incorporate different criteria from that designed to evaluate the sciences.

In proposing the extension of this idea into a nationally validated system for all 16 year olds to replace the Secretary of State's present proposals, it may well be that a standard weighting should be agreed between schools for any particular attribute. For example, a student's ability to apply his knowledge in a new context should be given the same weighting in all science profiles. What should be flexible, however, is the syllabus content. If there is to be a common core in a subject, teachers would retain a large measure of autonomy in selecting the remainder. This content could then be responsive to students' interests, to local circumstances and to industry's needs. This would be a genuine attempt to introduce relevance and responsiveness to change, both of which have featured largely in recent curriculum debates.[7] Such flexibility is at present impossible since teachers depend on changes determined by the examinations boards. These changes, moreover, frequently reflect the interests of university academics as chief examiners rather than the changing national economic or local community conditions in which young people find themselves. As a consequence students are often ill-equipped, through their present school knowledge and skills, to meet these conditions outside the classroom.

The question is whether it is practicable to implement this proposal. Initially the innovation may seem too radical, partly because it embraces all 16 year olds and not just the 60 per cent previously deemed of GCE and CSE potential, and partly because of the moderation of this form of assessment. However, the actual procedures necessary for implementation are already in existence. We would extend these procedures by changing the function of existing examiners and their assistants, and recognising more fully the evaluative role of teachers. Existing examining boards now nationally validating and standardising GCE O levels and CSE could extend their function to become validating bodies for the weighting system of the profiles, for example by agreeing that between two schools students' creativity in English should be evaluated similarly. With these boards too would be the responsibility for agreeing a core syllabus. Their assessment function would, however, be restricted to moderating the teachers' assessments of student performance, thereby guaranteeing uniformity of standards and conferring 'objectivity' on the subjectively formulated profiles.

Conclusions

Inevitably these proposals will meet resistance, but the grounds of this opposition should be carefully examined. On the positive side the scheme offers a more over-arching, finer instrument of assessment than that now employed for 16 year olds. It provides a diagnostic tool for teachers and a more accurate predictive tool for selectors. Secondly the proposal is non-divisive in embracing all 16 year olds. It would not produce a 'submerged' group as at present. On the issue of standards, discussion centres on ways of conferring objectivity. It has been argued earlier that the methods advocated are no less objective than those at present used in O level. The fear that the quantity of work to be moderated will be unwieldy can be and should be met administratively, if the system of statements can be shown to be advantageous to students, schools and society. This is why, before launching this proposal nationally, it is crucial to establish further its feasibility within several schools. We await the results of pilot projects currently under way, which could serve to demonstrate the positive value of this alternative to external examinations.

References

1 Whitehead, J., *Improving Learning for 11–14 year olds in mixed ability science groups*, Wiltshire Curriculum Centre, 1976, p. 6. This report describes how a group of teachers moved from class-based teaching, which denied the opportunity for enquiry learning, to individual and small group learning which allowed this opportunity

2 For example the team of science teachers coordinated by Martin Hyman at Hreod Burna School, Swindon in Wiltshire

3 The Avon Resources for Learning Unit was established in 1974 by the DES and Avon County to explore the claims made for resource-based learning. Resources and details of organisational methods are now available from: The Avon Resources for Learning Unit, Redcross Street, Bristol, BS2 OBA (Tel. 0272/559491)

4 See 1

5 See p. 16 in 1 above

6 This profile was developed by Maggie Hannon and Tony Cole at Wootton Bassett School, Swindon

7 *Education in Schools*: A Consultative Document, HMSO, 1977

4 The Record of Personal Experience

DON STANSBURY

A boy examined

An examination is a way of throwing light into dark places. It is a kind of revelation. As we look at a class we see thirty heads bent over their desks. As we mark their papers we judge how they are getting on. We translate this knowledge into symbols and we send it off to parents and future employers or we store it so that it can be found whenever anyone needs it.

As we go through this well-worn ritual we sometimes wonder if we are sufficiently examining ourselves and our own purposes. Is the light that we are directing at these young people serving only to dazzle and confuse them whilst leaving our own intentions and actions unexamined in the darkness?

One way of approaching this question is to take one boy – one of those bent heads – and to consider how the information which examinations will give us squares with other information that we can obtain about him. Before he came to his secondary school this boy was classified as remedial. On the basis of tests of intelligence, of reading and of numeracy he was placed at the age of 11 in a remedial class of thirteen pupils who were in fact the weakest in an age group of 300. He worked hard and did well and after a while was moved into a larger group of semi-remedial pupils. He continued to do well and got excellent reports from his teachers but there was never a case for moving him further up the ladder into the lower band of his comprehensive school.

He was a shy, rather solitary boy. He did not like playing football or messing about with friends. He lived in a very small village. His parents were not wealthy but he was always sent to school looking clean and in well-kept school uniform. Clearly, sacrifices were being made by a family that was proud of having decent standards and that was very caring and close to one another. His teachers who knew him well and were very pleased to have such a good student felt that his nature was best suited to the protected environment of a class for slow learners.

At the end of five years of secondary education he had examination results to show that he was above average in art, below average in maths and average in English, metalwork, woodwork and social studies. His reports all stressed how hardworking and willing and cooperative he had been and from all this a clearly defined and very familiar picture emerges.

There the evidence would rest if he had not also written a record of his own experience of his education which I have been privileged to read and which casts a new light on the whole process of his education as it appears to him and as it involves him and his teachers and his parents. As soon as I began to read his record I could feel the presence of a strong, independent intelligence – not the ability to pass intelligence tests but the personal quality that people reveal when they solve problems set by their environment, make intelligent choices or sort out and master the mass of experience that is their lives. Unfortunately, it is not a quality that is often required of school children. On the whole they are not expected to take decisions or make choices. The kind of learning that children do in school can require a high mental capacity but it does not often demand or develop intelligence. When they are asked questions they are not expected to think about them but to follow an agreed procedure which will lead to the correct answer. The idea that there is always a correct answer and that it is to be found at the back of the teacher's book is inhibiting to the development of intelligence, and for this reason I have tended to feel that this quality is unlikely to be found in a hardworking, conformist, obedient student in a class for slow learners.

But I have been wrong. The pattern of working and of behaviour that this boy has adopted is shown by his record to be an intelligent response to the circumstances of his life. He has done his best because that is clearly the best that he can do, given the fact that he has to be in school.

Most of his record, however, like most of the records I have read, is about education out of school. He recounts a walk with his father which was his first experience of a great expanse of open, uninhabited, unfenced country with all its attendant dangers of sudden mists, bogs and mine shafts. Then he recounts a walk with his brother and then a walk alone. This is dangerous and he knows it is and prepares carefully. He is very well equipped and is clearly competent with map and compass and has a proper survival kit. He prepares his route and leaves it with his parents, who clearly accept and know what he is doing. One card in his record describes how he walked all day alone through heavy mist by compass and kept unerringly to his route and to his time. My own view is that people should not do this. I believe it is too dangerous and could put other lives at risk, but it is clearly a challenge and a persistent demand on the intelligence. Wrong answers will not be corrected by an always right and protective teacher; in this activity they may be punished by experience. A boy who sets out to do this has to plan, to anticipate and to make choices and decisions. The school experience of waiting for the teacher to say what will be done today is very far away. It is possible that if school required children to plan, to make decisions, to show initiative and responsibility, this lad would not need to find that experience for himself alone and high up on the hills. Maybe we should allow more people to risk themselves. It is possible that the mass of idle, undirected, unmotivated youths who spend their time watching television are more at risk and may present more problems and fewer opportunities to the community than does this boy as he carefully charts his way from high point to high point on the hills.

Within six months of his first experience of these solitary places he is recording a three-day camp with his brother. Then in November he is camping alone. This is certainly dangerous and very demanding in all sorts of ways. A person who can do it must have certain qualities that are quite rare but are much needed.

This boy's record reveals something very important about him and it also casts a very useful light on the whole business of schooling. We may conclude that what he is doing on the hills is unwise and wrong but we could also conclude that what we are doing with boys and girls of such various talents and capacities in our classrooms is unwise and wrong. There may be much less likelihood that this boy will lose himself on the hills than that many other children will lose themselves in our classrooms. We all have to face the very real danger that we are now producing a race of mindless and thoughtless robots, who will be replaced by mechanical robots and so left with nothing to do except exist and consume.

Our school examination system is preparing children for a society and a technology that has almost completely vanished. It is clear that the whole thrust of current technology is to reduce the value of memorised knowledge and of learnt mechanical skills. At the same time it raises the value and increases the importance of all those things that machines and data stores cannot do. The most dangerous thing that we can do with children at this time is to programme them so that they all have the same responses, the same inability to question, to judge and to decide. Schools must develop in students their human attributes so that people can do the things that machines cannot do. This means encouraging flexibility and variety and putting a proper emphasis on the development of all kinds of personal qualities. This cannot be achieved through a system of instruction and examination alone, but a properly organised system of personally compiled records would help.

Personally compiled records

There is not room here to describe the inquiries, the arguments, the experiments that led by 1970 to the design, manufacture and use in several schools of the Record of Personal Achievement, and to the development, some years later, of the Record of Personal Experience, Qualities and Qualifications.

At the heart of both systems was the idea of personally compiled records. Although not in itself a new idea we had found an alternative to the idea of certification or accreditation. Many people when they apply for jobs draw up a statement of experience or of achievements. This is a personally compiled record. Like the RPA and the RPE it documents personal qualifications both through the items themselves and through the selection of items. It shows the kind of person the compiler wishes to be. It is a declaration of identity.

While it is not possible to motivate or qualify everyone through an examination or a system of reports, anyone can compile a personal record and this can relate to any kind of job and express any set of values.

The RPA was designed to be compiled over a period of two years. Items were recorded on loose leaf cards and kept in a four post binder. Each pupil also had a diary. Each week he would discuss with his tutor the items he had put into his diary and then transfer some items on to record cards to put into his record book. There were twenty-nine different designs of record card, and hopefully these could accommodate any record that any pupil wished to make.

Of course many people could not accept the idea that the Record of Personal Achievement could be a qualification. This was because they could only think in terms of one kind of qualification which was, of course, the familiar paper qualification to which our schools remain almost solely directed. People readily accept the idea that, for instance, Grade I CSE in English Literature is a qualification for a motor mechanic. However, people are not qualified for employment only by the examinations they have taken. They are also qualified by their qualities, their character, their interests and their attitudes. A boy who is strong, hardworking, reliable and interested in cars could be better qualified to become a motor mechanic than a boy who lacks these characteristics but has a Grade I CSE in English Literature. The failure of so many people to grasp this obvious point and to act upon it before the raising of the school leaving age has been a cause of our present problem of juvenile unemployment.

At an interview for a job, a personally compiled record has a varying degree of usefulness.

One of the first people to take a record book to an interview was a girl from a special school for educationally subnormal pupils. She went to a hotel to get a job washing up. She was dreadfully shy and inarticulate. She pushed her book across the desk, and so made contact with the adult on the other side, got the job and deserved to get it because her shyness was no disqualification for that work. She came back to school triumphant.

At a higher level a record will reveal qualities of character. One boy recorded:

Making up a bicycle.
I made up a bicycle for myself. I got the frame off a friend of mine. Then I painted it red and white. I bought a pair of handle bars, back wheel and two tyres. I found the seat, the stem and the front wheel in a dump. I then put all that on and I had some brakes and fitted them on and made sure they work all right. Then I put a dynamo on and put some new bulbs in the lights.

This was signed by his father. It shows an interest and an aptitude, but it also shows determination and initiative. These are important qualities and they are revealed by the things that people do. A record of experience can reveal qualities and characteristics in this way and for this reason it can be a most useful document for a prospective employer.

The best way to understand the essential characteristics of a personally compiled record is to read a record book. At first it is all unfamiliar and strange. It looks like a catalogue of trivial and haphazard experiences and events. It is clearly not a diary or an autobiography. It is not organised under headings like a *curriculum vitae*. It is not a self-assessment or any kind of self-composed report or self-examination. It has a random quality which many readers are going to find hard to grasp. It is very difficult to approach such a record for the first time with an open mind and simply to ask the question 'What does this show about the person who made it?'

In June 1978, teachers from six schools using the RPE met at Nottingham University to find out how much useful information could be taken from a personally compiled record by a complete stranger who had no other source of information about the recorder. Each school provided at least one record book and these were copied by the University so that we could all read simultaneously. We then pooled the information that we got from the record about the interests, aptitudes and personal qualities of the recorder. While we did this the teacher who knew the recorder kept silence. The result was astonishing. In every case the picture was true and in two cases it was almost uncannily accurate in depth and detail. This exercise seemed to provide strong evidence that reading a record book can give reliable information about personal qualities. What is not proved, however, is whether anyone who is not familiar with the idea of personally compiled records can get much information from it. What has to be accepted is that the record book contains primary unprocessed material. It does not provide ready-made assessments in any kind of processed form. It is the raw material for an assessment by the reader in the light of his own experience and powers of judgement.

Some of the people who doubted the reliability of a personally compiled record as documentary evidence of personal qualifications did so because they feared that students would falsify their records in order to gain an advantage. In order to reduce this possibility we stipulated that every item had to be signed by an adult who knew it to be true. Experience has shown, however, that this is not a problem. I have been astonished by the integrity of these records. I remember a boy who decided to record the fact that he had only been absent twice in the course of a school year and to get this signed by his form teacher. She found that according to the class register he had not been absent at all but he insisted on having it right in his record. I have been surprised by integrity of this kind, especially when it had come from people whom I have known to cheat in other ways. I have concluded that it occurs because people see in their own record a statement of their own identity and they do not want this to be untrue. In order to tap this emotion, the record must be completely personal. The items must be freely chosen by the recorder and expressed in his or her own way.

Recording is not only of benefit to the less able but is something which can be of value to anyone. It is important for all adolescents to ask themselves who are they, what are their skills and aptitudes? In what circumstances do they prosper? In what ways can they contribute to other people? What work can they do? Recording can help young people to define themselves and to direct themselves in a positive and constructive and optimistic way. If every young person made a record during the two years prior to leaving school it would give them all a greater sense of direction and purpose; it would improve attitudes and reduce alienation; it would correct the tendency of schools to devalue manual and mechanical work and it would give employers access to reliable and usable information about personal qualities and about character.

The Record of Personal Experience was first introduced in 1974 at King Edward VI Comprehensive School, Totnes, Devon. Its development has been inhibited by the absence of any public support or finance but it has operated very successfully at Totnes and has been adopted by six schools in the Nottingham area, where it has kept going because of the interest of Nottingham University and the existence at the University of a Working Party on RPE which brings together and encourages the teachers involved.

The design of the Record of Personal Experience has led to three significant findings. The first is that it is possible, because of a better arrangement of materials and because of good quality support materials for tutors, to cope with between twenty and thirty pupils at once. This makes recording practical in the normal school situation. The idea and technique of group tutoring and the arrangement of materials that was introduced in 1977 has been of assistance to this.

A significant advance has also been made in the use of recording by able students. A record that states '*I started writing poetry about three years ago and in that time I have written about 225 poems*' shows something significant about an able pupil. Although recording has so far been done mainly by pupils who are unsuccessful in terms of school examinations, there is no reason why all kinds of people should not be involved. Recording is a very adaptable form. The records made by Chinese and Indian pupils in Nottingham schools have shown how this system can be appropriate to a variety of cultures.

What now needs to be done is for a system, or a number of systems, of personally compiled records to be introduced in all secondary schools for students between the ages of 14 and 16. This would enable every student to leave school or to enter further education with a personally compiled record. Of course this would not be the only form of documentation for school leavers. There would still be a need for examinations or assessments of some kind, and for reports or testimonials or confidentials. The personally compiled records would have to be clearly separate and distinct from any document based on assessment. The two things could not be bound up in one document.

I believe that a properly organised system of personally compiled records in all schools would complement and support whatever system of assessment or of reporting or profiling people may be used. By removing some of the pressures that are at present perverting and confusing the business of documentation at 16 plus it would improve the health of our schools, of the economy and of society.

5   The Sutton Centre Profile

COLIN FLETCHER

This chapter takes the form of an analysis of arguments and a discussion of some of the relevant facts concerning profiles at Sutton Centre. This is not to say that I do not have strong opinions, or that I am not reasonably convinced profiles can and do work. This book, however, offered an opportunity to account for some research into practice and to show the way in which polemics are in fact part of a broader problem.

The following four sections are meant to give the reader some understanding of the school, the bare bones of the profile system, a little of what I have learned from conversations with tutors and their students, and the way in which the profiles can be said to answer serious criticisms. To begin with, Sutton Centre is a Community School, and profiles are part of a grounded alternative. To be a Community School means more than having a progressive pedagogy, curriculum and structure: it means that community is part of all three, and it means being as far-thinking, democratic and egalitarian as possible. Profiles play an integral part in the life of a Community School. In fact, they only become an end in themselves when they are challenged or being written about as distinct entities. The proposition is that less human modes of assessment would be the seeds of alienation. Non-alienative education is the goal, although some may set their sights higher and in more positive tones. At Sutton Centre all assessment is continuous, CSE Mode III examinations serve as assessments of the students' ability in subjects, and profiles record a three-way communication on the whole person. In essence, profiles are a matter of students, parents and teachers writing about and to each other.

Sutton Centre began its profile system in 1972 and it has been developed by significant documentation, some of which will be used later. Guidelines are given to staff in the annual pack of papers, and at the time of writing there is a working party to discuss the first full generation of experience. Students and staff are critical, particularly in the later years at school. Their criticisms offer the basis of revision, and the criticisms from within are more serious than those from without.

As Sutton Centre has already been the subject of two enquiries, this good school has had to explain the ways in which it is good. In the appropriate section the questions will simply be raised and dealt with. At this point it is important to realise that they are the slights and arrows of outrageous fetishists. By constantly having to deal with doubts about the needs of employers, high flyers and unexceptional staff it is made apparent that people do not think they need to go much further than have doubts. To be sure these questions do not all come from the same source but they do have the same tones: the belief that there is a fatal flaw in the argument, which means that it does not have to be examined in its own terms.

Sutton Centre as a community school

The feasibility study which gave rise to the idea of the Centre was carried out in 1970–71. A group of Chief Officers of the County Council interviewed a great many people in the area and what emerged was that the town, as such, was lacking in focus. Like a wheel without a hub, it was fragmented. It was necessary to create a centre of amenities that would enliven the town and attract growth. Coincidentally, there was an immediate need to build a comprehensive school ultimately for 1200 students. The Chief Education Officer and County Architect developed the notion of a community school in a community centre, combining Leisure Centre, Youth Services, Teachers' Centre, Careers Office, Day Centre, LEA Adult Education, WEA/University Extra-mural and Adult Literacy with statutory education, thereby mixing adult and child education.

This notion of community education was by no means original, but the combination of the school in a leisure and amenity centre, adjacent to a shopping precinct and a market place, was a unique idea. The important feature of the educational programme was first stated in the feasibility report: 'If education in school is to be a preparation for life, we see no fundamental difference between education and social education.' In brief there was to be a positive code of conduct. Once adults and children can work together on the business of learning, education has moved from its status as a childhood activity to that of a part of everyday life.

The public thoroughfare through the centre ensures that there are adults outside as well as within. In return, school must look outward for much of its subject matter. It is a responsibility of teachers to be fully aware of local events, activities and resources and to help school students to share that awareness and use it. Education, by its very nature, serves to integrate the community, and also to develop it, in equipping young and old to understand their social environment, their relations to it and their creative potential within it. This much was foreseen both by the feasibility study group, and by Stewart Wilson, the man they chose to achieve the working out of these ideas in the school at Sutton Centre.

What was done was to construct a curriculum that in some way covered all aspects of the life of the individual student in Sutton in 1973, and to develop means of teaching to that curriculum. Broad headings emerged which lent themselves to the concept of a block timetable: a timetable which meant studying each subject once a week in a continuous session equivalent to half a day. This was an immense asset in reducing the institutional atmosphere of the school. It also prepared the way for suspended weeks: weeks when the whole school timetable was abandoned, and numerous special interest options would be offered by staff members for recreation, project work, catch-up work with CSE, community work and craft activities.

The tutor group system of mixed ability teaching in a fixed social family was introduced, the aim being that, allowing for a few alterations in the first or second year, the tutor group should be constant throughout the school career of each student and should be both the social and academic unit of school organisation. This, coupled with the home visit requirement that tutors must visit the families of their group twice a year at least, was intended to create a situation of developing relationships and commitments, away from the competitive reshuffling of banding and streaming. Each student and teacher would have an identity and responsibility, not merely as an individual with certain abilities in certain subjects, but within a group, and with a particular area of the school. All lessons would take place within that group, and the tutor would always have some teaching to do with them, as well as time with them for discussion, organisation and relaxation. With no staff room to retire to, tutors are always in the social world of the students.

The profiles

Profiles are substantial documents. Their bulk comes from being printed on card and the fact that practically everything of any relevance to the student is recorded on them. The Staff Prospectus carries the following guidelines:

Profile sheets should be organised into the correct order as follows:
1   a) Sutton Centre Information Sheet
*   b) Personal Section*
*   i) Personal information sheet – this sheet is prepared in the C. and R. Department.*
*   ii) Attendance – a record of attendance kept by the student.*
*   iii) Centre Activities – these sheets record activities of special interest which although based at or involving the Centre have usually taken place*

*outside the 9.00 a.m. to 4.00 p.m. session times, e.g. clubs, camps, outings
and work done in 11 Sessions.*

    iv) Other interests and activities.

2 *General commentary by the tutor.*

3 *Subject section in alphabetical order but with Basic Skills at the end.*

There should be three types of sheets in each subject:

    i) Departmental subject summary.

    *ii) Teacher's Comments Sheet – every sheet should have the correct title
and date, and each comment should be initialled and dated.*

    *iii) Record of activities sheets. These sheets are completed by the student
when actually working in the department concerned. They are, therefore,
kept for the most part by the appropriate Course Director.*

Subject sheets should be in the following order:

  1   *Communications & Resources*

  2   *Creative Arts*

  3   *Environmental*

  4   *European Studies*

  5   *Home Management*

  6   *Literature & Drama*

  7   *Maths*

  8   *Personal Relationships*

  9   *Science*

  10 *Sports & Leisure*

  11 *Technical Studies*

  12 *Basic Skills*

*There should be a sheet of coloured card separating sections 1/2, 2/3 and 3/4,
and between Technical Studies and Basic Skills.*

The same prospectus gives an example of a typical group tutor week and suggests that on Mondays, amongst other things, there would be writing into the profile of any special activities which had taken place over the weekend; and on Fridays there would be individual tutoring and discussion about the profile. The first impression, therefore, must be that this is intended to be a total document. It is not intended to be a collection of the creative writings or more personal thoughts of the young people concerned. Specifically the profile is the personal record and property of the student. At the same time, of course, this person is the centre of a dialogue between teacher and parent, as well as being a party to it. In fact, it becomes clear when specific sheets are read that who is communicating with whom is a basic issue. Most teachers write for the student, whilst a few write to the parent. Students decide whether or not they agree with the teachers' comments, and make resolutions. Then the parents would seem to reply to the teachers and chide or encourage their children more directly than many of the teachers have done in their comments.

Four examples follow, two referring to girls and their performance in literature, drama and mathematics and two referring to boys and their performance in art and European Studies. Finally there is one page of other interests and activities.

These examples have been typed to ensure confidentiality. Each actual profile sheet is completed in handwriting, each comment being signed and dated. The total profile contains perhaps 40 sheets bound in a substantial A4 size file.

1st Girl D
Lit. and Drama   *1973–74*

```
┌─────────────────────────────────────────────────────────────┐
│ Teacher's Comments                                            │
├─────────────────────────────────────────────────────────────┤
│ D's work is spoilt by her spelling and her inability to give  │
│ work in to be marked when it is finished.  She is imaginative │
│ but must organise herself to finish work and take a pride in  │
│ it.   It has taken her a long time to settle down at the Centre│
│ and I am sure will soon be forging ahead!                     │
│                           signed                              │
└─────────────────────────────────────────────────────────────┘
┌─────────────────────────────────────────────────────────────┐
│ Pupil's Comments                                              │
├─────────────────────────────────────────────────────────────┤
│ 15th July                                                     │
│ I agree with this coment.   my spelling is bad I will try and │
│ improve it.   This term in lit and drama has been quite       │
│ interesting                                                   │
│                           signed                              │
└─────────────────────────────────────────────────────────────┘
┌─────────────────────────────────────────────────────────────┐
│ Parent's Comments                                             │
├─────────────────────────────────────────────────────────────┤
│ D has been given a dictionary to help improve her spelling, she│
│ will be encouraged to use it and to be prompt in handing in   │
│ finished work                                                 │
│                           signed                              │
└─────────────────────────────────────────────────────────────┘
```

2nd Girl J
Mathematics

Teacher's Comments

J must learn to discipline herself to work according to the
pattern established.   She had a very slow start but has
improved later and now is making some progress.   She does not
find the subject easy and will have to work really hard at it.

signed   19.12.74

J, within the limits of her ability, has continued to make
progress.   She seems to be enjoying the work and recently has
done really well.   signed   12.7.75

Pupil's Comments

I will try to discipline my self and work harder in maths.   I
think it is a fier coment.   signed   17.1.75

I am pleased with this comment and I think I do enjoy the work
we do.   signed   24 July

Parent's Comments

Pleased J is making some progress in this subject.   I think she
has always found the subject hard.

signed

First Boy N
Art

Teacher's Comments

He worked competently without really working up a sweat.   You
could have put more into your module, N, if you had wanted.   You
have talent in the artistic field so don't be tempted to rest on
your laurels.

signed

Pupil's Comments

As I remember, I put a lot of work into this subject.   I came back
to four Art 11th Sessions, and did work at home.   My finished work
took a lot of time to get as I wanted it.   I spent a great deal
of time on shading – I did enjoy the lesson!

signed

Parent's Comments

Remember N when you have done your best, that is the time when you
start looking for further improvements

signed

2nd Boy P
European Studies   *1975/6*

```
┌─────────────────────────────────────────────────────────────────┐
│ Teacher's Comments                                                │
├─────────────────────────────────────────────────────────────────┤
│ P seems to have settled down quite well and he tries hard with his│
│ written work.   Keep concentrating, P, and you should learn a lot.│
│                            signed            Jan. '76.            │
│ He has continued to work well, and he is making good progress.    │
│                            signed            July '76.            │
└─────────────────────────────────────────────────────────────────┘
```

```
┌─────────────────────────────────────────────────────────────────┐
│ Pupil's Comments                                                  │
├─────────────────────────────────────────────────────────────────┤
│ I like European Studies because it is French and I like French    │
│ and European Studies and I like it because it is very good lesson  │
└─────────────────────────────────────────────────────────────────┘
```

```
┌─────────────────────────────────────────────────────────────────┐
│ Parent's Comments                                                 │
├─────────────────────────────────────────────────────────────────┤
│ I am Pleased with P's work as now he can Read better but he goes   │
│ to Fast with writing                 signed                       │
└─────────────────────────────────────────────────────────────────┘
```

Date	Other Interests and Activities
July	Myself and some of my friends are now making a film, which will be sent to the Screen Test competition. We are working on an idea set in Sherwood Forest. (It is also a part time school activity as well)
25.9.77	On Sunday John and myself went a bike ride to Selston and all round that district. On the way back it rained very hard and we both got wet through. We both had the misfortune of our front brake cable snapping!
1978	During the Whit holidays, John, Jack, Steve and myself spent some days camping in Bagthorpe. During our time camping there, we made a couple of films. One of them is an entry for the Screen Test Young film makers comp. The other film was one made just for our enjoyment and entertainment.

It was felt at first that the profiles would be the only reference needed when these young people sought employment. However, a single sheet entitled 'to whom it may concern' has since been prepared which gives a summary of the student's attendance and punctuality records, courses followed and personal development.

The profiles have emerged as having particular importance in relation to follow-up work, continuous effort, and dealing with weaknesses rather than complementing strengths. In fact, the part of the process to which they could especially refer is that often treated as the problems of adolescents. It is clear from sample reading that students often begin their profiles with extensive illustration and drawing, but that this practice tends to die out by the age of 13 or 14. Although not a direct commentary on adolescence it is important that what began as a full-blown experiment in expression can be quite acceptably reduced to a skeleton process when there are other pressing preoccupations. This acceptance may be in part because many tutors realise that they may have expected too much of their students and have consciously relaxed their demands.

Discussions on profiles

Discussions with fifth form students, that is with those who have passed right through the system and are now nearing the end, suggest that a number of major problems have crept into the practice of the profile system. The first is that the profile work is mandatory and this makes it a chore. They feel that the profiles are too demanding. Although their parents read them and wrote comments extensively in their early years, they may respond now with a signature only. Some students ask for a more creative emphasis: they want to be able to keep their best work, rather like the portfolio of the would-be art college student. Students see the profile as having real value as a private document between themselves and their own tutor. Having no knowledge of report systems and the importance with which reports are regarded by some parents, they are not in a position to make comparisons between one-way and three-way communications. They did, however, say that the two main consequences of reading comments from parents were either to be pleasantly surprised or to be encouraged to greater efforts. The students did not object to doing profiles but to doing too much, too often and compulsorily. In brief, they wanted to produce a document in which they could have more pride.

The teachers' working party on profiles has taken up these and related problems. The first is the confusion about who is writing to whom. It is felt that teachers must make this clear and talk about this with parents while making home visits. Secondly, the record of activity cards appeared to expect too much. Instead of writing about their reflections students would rather get on with the lesson. So far, however, there has been no wish to go further than to clarify the profiles. The three-way communication is to remain whilst greater emphasis will probably be placed upon that between the student's tutor and the parent, and less will be expected from the communication between subject tutors and the parents. This should allow more of the students' energies to be directed towards records of personal experience based upon Don Stanbury's accounts of the Swindon project, and meet the separate demand for a private archive of the best creative work. In all probability, therefore, some six years of experience are leading to reform rather than rejection of the profile system. If the system is thus strengthed, it should cope better with hostile criticisms.

Criticisms and some responses to them

The primary purpose of profiles is to help school students to develop their full potential. Students are encouraged by the use of profiles to think about and learn from their own actions, to become attuned to adult criticism and to respond to it, and to undertake extensive writing practice. When the student reaches the age of 16, however, the question arises: will anyone read his profile?

Interviews with local employers have produced the bald statement that they devote a maximum of fifteen minutes to considering a case, and that they place greater emphasis upon an interview than they do upon any written material. The few who are prepared to persevere with profiles are those who have had direct contact as parents. Perhaps it should be said that the local job market is good for the 16 plus age group. There is work particularly in hosiery and light engineering, although it may not be what young people really want or can fully manage. Analysis of the school's previous leavers shows that there is a great deal of movement between the ages of 16 and 18 as youngsters gradually establish where the best money is paid. In other cases, the power of parents and relatives has been used in securing a good opening and the chance of a trade. In the small town of Sutton-in-Ashfield 80 per cent of employment is in the manual grades although it has also a small service sector. For these reasons, unless the young person is of an academic inclination, profiles and formal assessment have little value in the local job market.

So what about high flyers?

Until very recently there was little or no expectation of O levels and A levels. A sixth form is new to the town. Now there are some thirty-six pupils in the first year sixth, all with some CSEs and some with A levels. That some A levels have already been gained (and with excellent grades) by students in the first year sixth is attributed to independent learning. Profiles cannot be said to have caused such attainment! Profiles have, however, played a part in the social development of the academically gifted; the obverse is therefore of equal importance at Sutton Centre. The staff accept that there will be academic high flyers who attain A levels at a considerably earlier age than is usually expected and they are concerned that these pupils do not become 'swots' and socially maladjusted in the process.

Is it not possible that such systems only work when there are young, committed and talented staff?

Sadly it is possible to test this proposition, as seventeen members of staff left one term after Stewart Wilson had departed to open a new Community School in West Lothian, Scotland. Critics hoped that they would be replaced by more local and more traditional teachers who would change the system. But local and traditional or not, the new staff have continued the process. The point really is that engaging in profile systems is a matter of culture rather than of competence; if that is what is expected by the codes of the school, then teaching staff try it and try to make it work.

In research now under way to test some of the propositions which it has been possible to make so far, the focus is upon the process of doing profiles rather than upon profiles as a product. The propositions read as follows:

Continuous assessment shared between student, parent and tutor is good educational practice in any school and an essential part of a community school.

Secondly, when this assessment is a three-way responsibility it facilitates social development whilst measuring it; if approached with any degree of thought or integrity whatsoever all parties change towards each other and within themselves.

6 The Scottish Pupil Profile System

PATRICIA BROADFOOT

Every chapter in this book is about the inadequacy of existing certification procedures for 16 year olds. Each chapter explores one of a number of possible alternative procedures that have been developed to provide more informative school records – informative in the sense that they can provide a worthwhile and realistic educational goal for all pupils, whilst at the same time communicating reliable and useful information for potential employers and tertiary education. This chapter describes one such alternative method of 16 plus certification developed in Scotland, 'the pupil profile', and, in so doing, amplifies the argument that a radical re-thinking of methods of certification is possible and necessary and indeed long overdue.

An historical overview

The system of school certification in Scotland[1] has not changed substantially since the Scottish Education Department introduced 'Highers' in 1888. Since at this time the secondary school population was very small and destined mainly for further study at a university for professional occupations, the academic orientation and level of difficulty of the certification examinations was neither inappropriate in terms of content nor divisive as a selection mechanism since the goal it provided was within the grasp of the majority of the pupils who were able to stay on at school to take the examinations. With the gradual expansion of secondary education to more and more pupils and the associated increase in the length of compulsory schooling which has taken place over the last hundred years, the formal academic curriculum and the university-oriented certificate examinations have become increasingly anachronistic. Not long after the institution of universal secondary education in 1945, the Advisory Council Report on Secondary Education made public their recognition of the distortion that external examinations was creating in the curriculum of the secondary school.[2] They recommended instead the institution of a School Certificate based on *internal* examinations for (post compulsory) 16 year old school leavers who were not going to stay on at school to take the third 'Higher' level external examination which would remain as the qualification necessary for university entrance. The recommendations fell on deaf ears.

The group leaving certificate of four or five higher or lower passes – normally equated with successful completion of secondary education – was retained. Thus, as recently as the 1950s when all pupils were obliged to be in school until they were 15, it continued to be gained by less than 10 per cent of the age group. Two out of three pupils admitted to certificate courses were unsuccessful. The alternative 'Junior Leaving Certificate' more on the lines of the Advisory Council recommendations, which was run on a county basis and administered by individual schools, was of little value as it had no national currency and was in content a pale imitation of, rather than a genuine alternative to, the School Certificate.[3] In their report of 1955 on Junior Secondary Education, the Scottish Education Department deliberated possible alternatives.[4] Rather than looking for ways of broadening certification to include a greater range of both academic and non-academic school achievements of more relevance to many pupils and employers than those qualities that can be measured by formal written examinations, the Scottish Education Department chose instead to extend the scope of the traditional external examinations to a greater, *but still relatively small proportion* of the year group. The new 'Ordinary Grade' Scottish Certificate of Education instituted in 1962 was aimed at 16 year olds such that 'a pupil who is at the lower end *of the top 30 per cent* of any age group should, with satisfactory teaching and adequate effort on his part, have a reasonable prospect of securing passes in the O Grade in at least three subjects.[5]

The similarity of these recommendations to those in England of the Beloe Committee in 1960 as described by Burgess and Adams in Part I above are striking. The fact that by 1955 over 50 per cent of pupils in the secondary modern school were being presented for GCE O level examinations in at least one subject testified not only to the demise of the 'equal but different' ideal for the 'modern' school, envisaged in the tripartite division of the 1944 Education Act, but even more significantly to the intense pressure from the mass of secondary school population to have at least some chance of gaining a nationally recognised qualification. Recognising this pressure, the Beloe Report recommended new examinations to be taken in 4 or more subjects by candidates in the next 20 per cent below the 20 per cent who were expected to attempt GCE O level in 4 or more subjects.[6] Although a further 20 per cent might attempt individual subjects, nearly half the age group was to be denied the chance to achieve formal, public recognition for any achievement – academic or personal – during their school career.

With comprehensivisation and the raising of the school leaving age to 16 in 1972 this pressure on certification mechanisms intensified still further. Predictably this has led both in England and in Scotland to a demand, once again, for an extension of the range of 16 plus certification. In England these demands have taken the form of pressures to amalgamate GCE O level and CSE certification into a common system of examining at 16 plus.[7] In Scotland, the emphasis has been more on extending the existing 'common' (i.e. only) system. In 1973 the O Grade was 'banded' for the first time into levels of pass, ostensibly to allow more pupils to achieve some kind of award whilst maintaining differentiation between high and low achievers. However since bands D and E are known to represent marks of between 40–49 and 30–39 per cent respectively, public opinion very quickly came to regard these awards as failures in much the same way as the lower grades of CSE are regarded in England. That the banding of the O grade has not provided any solution to the problem of certification for the majority of statutory-age school leavers in Scotland is evidenced by the fact that fewer than two in three O grade presentations are successful (band C or over) and indeed that the proportion of successes has actually gone down from 76% in 1969 to 61.9% as presentation has gone up.[8] Local initiatives in instituting CSE examinations run by English boards and in the development of local school leaving certificates have served rather to underline the existing inadequacies of the system than to overcome them in any significant sense. Indeed, the continuing inadequacy of certification procedures in secondary education was recognised by the Secretary of State for Scotland in the setting up in 1974 of a prestigious committee to review assessment in the third and fourth years of secondary education in Scotland. Their report *Assessment for All*, published in 1977, draws the Scottish and English debates over 16 plus certification yet closer together in their mutual proposals for a solution to the problem of comprehensive 16 plus certification in the institution of an expanded version of traditional 16 plus examining.

As yet those current proposals for reform both in England and in Scotland are still the subject of debate. Meanwhile, certification continues to be totally inadequate. If one considers that of the 78.8% of the year group who were presented for SCE O grade examinations in 1974 the pass rate was only 61.9% and that included all those highly successful pupils who achieved as many as nine or ten passes, there is a very significant number of pupils who are leaving school without any qualification and whose predominant experience of school is one of being squeezed into courses which are too difficult and irrelevant or, alternatively, of being labelled 'non-certificate' and, by implication, 'system reject'. Although in England the problem is slightly less acute than in Scotland with the existence of CSE Mode III examination,[9] the value of this qualification suffers from its following in the lower status, internal examination, school report tradition of the Local Leaving Certificate. It is important to point out, however, that not only are the *existing* certification procedures inadequate in an age of comprehensive secondary education, but also the proposed innovations of the Schools Council in England and the Dunning Committee in Scotland for a common system of examining at 16 plus will do nothing to redress the situation. It is the central argument of this book that reforms which fall short of fundamental changes in the content and practice of 16 plus certification are merely fingers in the dyke. The retention of the single subject examination probably at different syllabus levels implies too the retention of the traditional secondary school emphasis on academic success, on its characteristic hierarchical structure, and a continued disregard for publicly recording the achievements of pupils in non-academic areas. Thus without much more fundamental changes than those currently proposed, the comprehensive school will remain an ideal rather than a reality for the large numbers of pupils whose aspirations and abilities do not accord with the anachronistic ethos of the secondary school. As a result, these pupils will continue to regard education as irrelevant and to be the despair of those who have to teach them.

The pupil profiles project

The lack, in current proposals for reform, of any serious attempt to provide a genuinely comprehensive system of 16 plus certification through a major change in emphasis has come to be widely recognised by educationists in Scotland and has resulted in a variety of localised initiatives seeking some more just certification procedure. One of the most significant of these initiatives resulted from the formation, under the auspices of the Head Teachers' Association of Scotland, of a nationally oriented Working Party on school assessment which sought both to develop and evaluate some alternative assessment procedure. The extent of concern was reflected in the membership of the Working Party which included, as well as head teachers, representatives from tertiary education, colleges of education, employers, local authorities and Her Majesty's Inspectorate. Its aims were incorporated into a research and development project supported by the Scottish Education Department and conducted by the Scottish Council for Research in Education. All agreed that what was needed was 'a procedure which would be equally applicable to all pupils; which would gather teachers' knowledge of pupils' many different skills, characteristics and achievements across the whole range of the curriculum, both formal and informal; which would, with the minium of clerical demands, provide a basis for continuing in-school guidance, culminating in a relevant and useful school-leaving report for all pupils.'[10] The record would include a variety of abilities and qualities that are not normally formally recorded, so that as well as necessary information on academic achievement and basic skills, credit would be given, for example, for perseverance and creativity, for helping other people through social service, for qualities of leadership shown in outdoor pursuits, for contributions to extra-curricular activities such as the school play or sport, or for just being a pleasant and helpful group member. Thus it was hoped that neither activities nor pupils would be categorised into 'certificate' and 'non-certificate' and, by implication, 'important' and 'not important', since it was felt that all areas of school life can contribute to personal development and thus all types of achievements have a value. Such a system, which recorded idiosyncratic achievements, would preclude a ready comparison between pupils and thus help to overcome the feelings of failure so inevitable when only one kind of achievement is acknowledged.

It was recognised too that the provision of an overall mark or grade in an activity is not helpful in diagnosing a pupil's strengths and weaknesses in order to help him make progress and that a 'profile' assessment — 'a set of data recording the scores of a student in respect of his performance over a range of items'[11] – would be much more useful both as a basis for in-school guidance for teachers, parents and pupils and for vocational guidance in giving both pupils and employers more information to help them make satisfactory choices. Thus the aim was to design an assessment system which would allow teachers to record their detailed knowledge of pupils' progress obtained in a variety of different ways, whether it be class work, tests or informal personal contact, and yet which would not put too heavy a clerical burden on the teacher in terms of form filling. These aims of the Working Party were in many ways contradictory. The need for detail, for example, as opposed to the need to avoid over-burdening teachers; the difficulty of being confident of reliability and fairness in what were inevitably often very subjective assessments; the difficulty of achieving comparability of standards between subjects and teachers in comments and grades are just a few of the more obvious problems.

However, by dint of trial and revision of early prototypes over a period of three years in a variety of Scottish comprehensive schools and with the help of extensive consultation with a great variety of interested parties, a recording and reporting system was developed which was felt by the Working Party to come as near as possible to meeting its original aims in a practicable way.

The SCRE profile assessment system

Briefly, the system involves three stages: first, collecting the teacher's assessments; secondly, their collation from class group sheets on to individual pupil records or 'profiles'; and thirdly, the production of a school leaving report based on the information provided in the profiles. Figure 6(i) (p. 62) shows the first stage of the process – the teacher's form. The form is divided into three sections, the first eight categories allowing for assessments to be made of each 'basic skill' of which the teacher feels she has knowledge for any pupil. Thus the English teacher would probably feel able to comment on 'listening', 'speaking', 'reading' and 'writing'. The outdoor pursuits teacher would perhaps have knowledge on 'listening' and 'speaking', 'visual understanding and expression' and 'physical co-ordination' for some if not all pupils. Grading is on a four-point scale based on criteria of achievement developed for each level of each skill by panels of teachers.[12] The next section, 'performance', is divided into two. The first part, as well as allowing for an overall 'composite' grading, provides a series of blank optional categories which allows teachers to define the important components of achievement in a particular activity, so that, in assessing individual pupils against these various components, they will be able to chart with which aspects of the activity the pupil is having difficulty or for which he is showing a particular talent. Again the four-point scale is used with criteria being devised by individual teachers or departments for each activity after the exemplars provided in the handbook.[13] The final section of the form is for the grading of the two work-related characteristics summarised as 'enterprise' and 'perseverance', which research has shown to have the highest predictive validity with occupational success in later life.[14] More idiosyncratic achievements and comments are recorded on the back of the class assessment sheet and transferred to the 'pupil profile' shown in Fig. 6(ii) (p. 63). When the class sheet has been filled in, the assessments from all the various class sheets are collated. This can be done by computer which collates together for each pupil the reports of all his or her teachers and prints them out on a pupil sheet. An alternative, manual system operates by having below the teacher's master-sheet a set of overlapping pupil sheets, on to the exposed edges of which the teacher's entries are reproduced by means of a carbon. These pupil slips can then be sorted and mounted for each pupil on a peg board (Fig. 6(ii)), such that a profile of the pupil is built up from the various teachers' assessments.

The school leaving statement

I have dwelt at some length on the first stage of the profile assessment process, emphasising within-school guidance, rather than on the reporting aspect of the procedure, which is more strictly relevant to the concerns

© Scottish Council for Research in Education 1976

S.C.R.E. PROFILE ASSESSMENT SYSTEM

CLASS ASSESSMENT SHEET

	Q. Quality	T. Johnson	F. Fielding	S. Roberts	F. Drake	H. Holmes	D. Kennedy	B. McGregor	R. James	L. Fraser	W. Jackson	F. Dunn	S. Smith	D. Gordon	D. Brown	K. McIntosh	P. Anderson	F. Law
Class Group	3L	3L	3L	3L	3L	3L	3L	3L	3L	3L	3L	3L	3L	3L	3L	3L	3L	3L
Skills — Listening	2	3	2	4	2	1	3	–	2	2	4	2	3	–	3	3	4	2
Speaking	2	4	1	3	3	2	3	2	2	4	4	1	1	3	3	1	4	2
Reading	1	2	2	3	2	1	2	2	3	2	3	2	3	2	3	4	3	1
Writing	2	3	1	4	3	1	3	2	4	2	4	2	4	3	4	4	4	2
Visual understanding & expression	4	3	1	3	4	3	2	2		1	3	3	3	3	2	3	4	2
Use of Number																		
Physical Coordination																		
Manual Dexterity			.	4		2					4			3				
Performance — Knowledge	1	4	3	4	3	1	4	2	3	4	3	3	4	1	3	4	1	1
Reasoning	2	3	2	3	2	1	3	1		2	4	3	3	2	4	4	1	1
Presentation	3	3	1	5	4	1		1	4	1	2	2	3	4	2	3	2	1
Imagination	2	4	1	1	3	2	2	2	1	3	4	2	1	3	3	3	2	2
Critical Awareness	2	3	2	2	4	1	3	2	1	2	4	2	2	2	4	4	4	2
Composite Grade	2	3	2	3	3	1	3	1	2	1	4	2	3	2	3	4	2	2
Perseverance	1	3	2	4	4	1	4	2	4	4	1	2	4	1	3	1	1	3
Enterprise	3	4	3	1	3	1	3	2	1	3	3	2	1	3	3	2	3	3
Subject/Activity	Hist.	Hist.	Hist.	Hist.	Hist.	Hist.	Hist.	Hist.	Hist.	Hist.	Hist.	Hist.	Hist.	Hist.	Hist.	Hist.	Hist.	Hist.
Teacher	JR Mc-G	JR Mc-G	JR Mc-G	JR Mc-G	JR Mc-G	JR Mc-G	JR Mc-G	JR Mc-G	JR Mc-G	JR Mc-G	JR Mc-G	JR Mc-G	JR Mc-G	JR Mc-G	JR Mc-G	JR Mc-G	JR Mc-G	JR Mc-G
Date	mar 1976 3/4	3/4	3/4	3/4	3/4	3/4	3/4	3/4	3/4	3/4	3/4	3/4	3/4	3/4	3/4	3/4	3/4	3/4

Figure 6(i)   Teacher Assessment Form

The duplicate copy underneath is a single sheet (computer version) or partially overlapping individual pupil sheets (manual version)

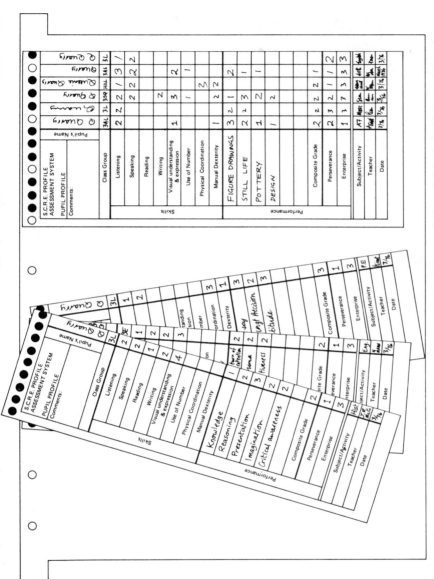

Figure 6(ii)   Manual mounting on a peg-board of assessment records relating to a single pupil. Records awaiting mounting are shown to the left. Each slip comes from a different teacher and is a duplicate of a single column of the teacher assessment sheet shown in Figure 6(i). Sorting and display can alternatively be done by computer.

SCHOOL LEAVING REPORT

This is a brief report on   Queenie Quarry

Date of Birth: 13/7/1960

who completed class   S4

in   Tanochbrae High   School

and left on   3rd July 1976

This report is the result of continuous assessment by all the teachers of this pupil and has the authority of:—

E P Smith   Head Teacher

J McGregor   Director

OTHER OBSERVATIONS

(includes other school activities, other awards and comments on positive personal qualities).

Royal Life-Saving Society – Bronze Medallion
Member School Photographic Club, School Debating Society
Member of School Skiing trip to Austria Jan 1976
She has been resourceful in finding costumes for the school play.
She has recently shown an appreciation and enjoyment of literature and has read widely outside the s llabus.
Works well on group activities; gets on well with both pupils and teachers. Readily accepts responsibility, particularly in school activities.

Notes

The grades A—D represent approximately 25% of the year group in each case.

The skill gradings represent a consensus derived from the individual ratings of each teacher's knowledge and reflect the standard obtained by the pupil with reasonable consistency.

All the information contained in this report is based on profile assessments contributed by each teacher on a continuous and cumulative basis, including observations of personal qualities and informal activities.

© 1976 SCRE

Figure 6(iii), a   An example of a completed school-leaving report using the form developed by the working party for the SCRE profile assessment system (pages 1 and 4)

SUBJECT/ACTIVITY ASSESSMENT

Curriculum Area	Subjects Studied (includes final year level where relevant)	Years of Study	Achievement	Enterprise (includes flair, creativity)	Perseverance (includes reliability, carefulness)
Aesthetic Subjects	Drawing	1–4	2	2	1
	Music	1–4	2	3	3
Business Studies					
Community/ Leisure Activities	Social Education	1–4	3	2	3
Crafts	Pottery	3–4	2	1	3
English	English	1–4	2	1	3
Mathematics	Arithmetic	1–4	1	1	2
Other Languages	German	2–4	2	2	3
Outdoor Studies	Outdoor Pursuits	3–4	2	2	3
Physical Education	General	1–4	3	1	3
Science	Biology	3–4	1	2	2
Social Subjects	History	1–4	2	1	3

SKILLS

LISTENING
- Acts independently and intelligently on complex verbal instructions ☐
- Can interpret and act on most complex instructions ☐ [TH]
- Can interpret and act on straightforward instructions ☐
- Can carry out simple instructions with supervision ☐

SPEAKING
- Can debate a point of view ☐
- Can make a clear and accurate oral report ☐ [TH]
- Can describe events orally ☐
- Can communicate adequately at conversation level ☐

READING
- Understands all appropriate written material ☐
- Understands the content and implications of most writing if simply expressed ☐ [TH]
- Understands uncomplicated ideas expressed in simple language ☐
- Can read most everyday information such as notices or simple instructions ☐

WRITING
- Can argue a point of view in writing ☐
- Can write a clear and accurate report ☐ [TH]
- Can write a simple account or letter ☐
- Can write simple messages and instructions ☐

VISUAL UNDERSTANDING AND EXPRESSION
- Can communicate complex visual concepts readily and appropriately ☐
- Can give a clear explanation by sketches and diagrams ☐
- Can interpret a variety of visual displays such as graphs or train timetables ☐
- Can interpret single visual displays such as roadsigns or outline maps ☐

USE OF NUMBER
- Quick and accurate in complicated or unfamiliar calculations ☐ [TH]
- Can do familiar or straightforward calculations, more slowly if complex ☐
- Can handle routine calculations with practice ☐
- Can do simple whole number calculations such as giving change ☐

PHYSICAL CO-ORDINATION
- A natural flair for complex tasks ☐
- Mastery of a wide variety of movements ☐
- Can perform satisfactorily most everyday movements ☐ [TH]
- Can perform single physical skills such as lifting or climbing ☐

MANUAL DEXTERITY
- Has fine control of complex tools and equipment ☐
- Satisfactory use of most tools and equipment ☐
- Can achieve simple tasks such as wiring a plug ☐ [TH]
- Can use simple tools, instruments and machines such as a screwdriver or typewriter ☐

Figure 6(iii), b   Pages 2 and 3 of the SCRE form

of this book. I have done so in order to emphasise two points: first, the importance of continuity between assessment *during* school and its culmination in a final report; and secondly, of having a system that is not only desirable but *practicable*. In this system the school leaving report can be built up from the information of profiles produced once or twice a year over several years, which have recorded important achievements by the pupil. The report, shown in Fig. 6(iii) (pp. 64 and 65), is the summation and abbreviation of the most recent internal assessments, giving more emphasis to achievement and omitting some of the diagnostic categories. It is envisaged that the pupil's house-tutor, guidance teacher or some other teacher who knows him well, would be responsible for interpreting and weighting the various assessments made by different teachers in order to identify, for example, basic skill ratings across a number of activities. Similarly such a teacher would be able to pick out the pupil's most significant achievements for inclusion in the 'other observations' section of the report. Essentially, the report is designed to be a summary of information which has formed the basis of a continuing dialogue between a pupil and his teachers.

The point has already been made that one of the factors which has bedevilled the widespread use of school-based reports in certification is their lack of national currency and comparability. In an effort to avoid this problem, great attention was paid in the design of the Pupil Profile Report as shown in Fig. 6(iii) to the question of moderation: the maintenance of comparability. The 'skills' section is designed to be as far as possible 'self-moderating', since very specific descriptions are offered of the standard achieved, the grade awarded being the composite of the assessments made by individual teachers.[15] The subject/activity assessment is the more traditional kind of report and it is envisaged that the grades entered here would be moderated by one of the Mode III type moderation procedures already developed. The back page of the report (shown in Fig. 6(iii), a) is the widest in scope, recording as it does the specific, idiosyncratic personal achievements and qualities of each pupil. This section could equally well include observations by the pupil himself. Thus, although not amenable to moderation, it is crucial if the report is to be genuinely comprehensive. The Pupil Profile Report can provide for all the existing 16 plus certification requirements while at the same time allowing for an equally positive statement to be achieved by less academic pupils.

Practicability, reliability and validity – a brief comment

It is useless to design a magnificent new system and then to find it does not work in practice. We must be sure that we can trust the assessments made, that the procedure is administratively feasible, and that it meets the appropriate needs. Thus an extensive evaluation exercise of the pupil profile assessment system was carried out simultaneously with the development work. Space does not permit me here to document in any detail the statistical tests made of the validity and reliability of the assessment procedure; of, for example, the way teachers used the assessment categories; how they distributed their grades and how far they agreed with one another in their assessment of basic skills – that is to say of the viability of converting the covert and informal assessment and observation constantly taking place in school activity into an overt, systematic profile. These data have been reported in detail elsewhere.[16] Certainly the analysis emphasised the value of profile assessment in revealing that teachers could and did distinguish in their assessments between the various aspects of achievement in an activity; and that as far as it was possible to discover within the limitations of a short-term research project there is every reason to believe that teachers' assessments built up over time are both more valid and more reliable than tests with respect to learning skills and most character qualities.

Extensive consultation with various interested parties – teachers, pupils, parents, employers and colleges of education – was generally favourable with respect to the central aims of the procedure: namely, to provide a report for *all* pupils containing information not only on academic attainment but on what, for many pupils, are more important factors: basic skills and personal qualities.

To innovate or not to innovate – some implications

In view of the near-unanimous support for the aims of the profile assessment procedure, it is perhaps surprising that a system of certification along these lines has not been instituted nationally or even recommended by the Dunning Committee in Scotland or the Schools Council in England. The reason for this lies in the contradictory and possibly irreconcilable demands currently being made on 16 plus certification and it is perhaps in making this situation apparent, as much as in its concrete suggestions for reform, that the Pupil Profile project can contribute to the 16 plus debate.

Until very recently research and development work on certification has been dominated by questions of technique – the 'how' of assessment. The first essential stage in designing a genuinely comprehensive certification system as the culmination of compulsory education is a change of focus in the debate away from 'how' towards a consideration of 'why' and 'with what effects'.[17] Unfortunately the several answers to these questions appear to be incompatible and thus the decisions made must be in terms of priorities. At the outset of this chapter I hinted at some of the incompatibilities encountered in designing the Profile Assessment procedure and thus of the.necessity of deciding priorities and making compromises. By setting out in a more general way some of the more obvious clashes in priorities in any decision about certification, I hope not only to explain the controversy that has surrounded the publication of the Pupil Profiles proposals, but also to clarify some of the issues that lie at the heart of this book.

The basic functions of 16 plus certification are threefold. First, provision for selection – comparing pupils on criteria of achievement in order to pick the most suitable or worthy candidates for tertiary education or particular jobs. Second, motivation – providing a goal for pupils to work towards; and third, control of standards within and between schools (and indeed to a great extent of curriculum content too). Certification will take various forms according to which of these central functions is given priority.

Forms of certification	*Functions of certification*		
	Motivation	*Selection*	*Control/ accountability*
no documentation	xxx		
pupil-compiled records	xxx		
'negotiated' pupil/ teacher records	x	x	x
external assessment		xx	x

x = some emphasis
xx = strong emphasis
xxx = exclusive emphasis

Figure 6(iv)   The contrasting emphases of alternative forms of certification

Figure 6(iv) summarises the options available in terms of these three functions. First, there is the possibility of no documentation. This would solve the problems of the reliability of assessments, would save a great deal of money currently spent on assessment and would, in theory, release teachers to pursue their own objectives and the interests of their pupils in complete freedom. Employers could be encouraged to develop their own relevant selection mechanisms (see Chapter 12 by Christina Townsend). Standards in schools could be maintained by other means, such as the Assessment of Performance Unit and by HM Inspectorate. The main disadvantages of such a system would seem to be the removal for pupils of a tangible goal in their education, which, in recognising their achievement, may encourage them to pursue their education further. Perhaps much more important, such a step simply would not be acceptable in today's society, since certification has come to be so heavily relied upon both inside and outside schools in encouraging motivation and allowing ostensibly fair selection. A hardly less radical alternative is that of self-compiled pupil records which again would release pupils from the hold of externally defined educational goals. Such records would be likely to encourage pupil motivation in relating to their own perspectives and provide valuable information for employers, but again, as the so-called 'Great Debate' clearly demonstrated, would be unlikely to find acceptance in the current educational and economic climate in which public opinion is demanding ever tighter controls on schools and educational objectives, particularly with regard to the development of basic skills. The lack of comparability in such records would make impossible one of the most important functions of existing 16 plus assessment: selection. Thus both these alternatives are likely to remain, at least for the time being, a dream of progressive educators and free schools. The contrast of this kind of record with the dominant traditional model of examination certification could hardly be more stark.

Two possibilities are left which provide some measure of compromise within the three different functions of certification: motivation, selection and accountability. The first is teacher-compiled profiles which, as has been shown in the Pupil Profile system, can record a wide range of pupil achievement and thereby encourage pupil motivation by recognising a diversity of educational goals. Such assessments, being made in accordance with generally agreed criteria and amenable to more informal methods of moderation, can also adequately fulfil public demands of comparability in instruments which are to be the basis of selection. The final, as yet largely untried, possibility is what might be called 'negotiated' records compiled jointly by teacher and pupil. Whilst inevitably still 'alienating' to some pupils in emphasising teacher and school definitions of achievement, unlike the pupil-compiled record in which the pupil himself decides which achievements are important to him, the negotiated record, in its very recognition that the pupil's perspective of his learning is important information to record, can serve to increase motivation.[18] Thus the 'negotiated' record may be the best compromise for 16 plus certification, since it removes the undesirable effects in the curriculum and on pupils of the purely academically-oriented external examination, whilst providing for selection and quality-control. At the same time, in recognising a variety of educational goals and in giving pupils a degree of responsibility in determining their own achievements, the negotiated record can provide a vital element of pupil self-respect. It is to be hoped that the development work of the Pupil Profiles project, which has found favour around the world, will be extended at the earliest opportunity to an examination of the potential of the 'negotiated' record. Only then will we even begin to approach a genuinely comprehensive 16 plus certification.

References

1 The arguments here are based on Scottish data since the Pupil Profiles project described in this chapter was set in Scotland but the picture for England is essentially similar

2 *Secondary Education* a report of the Advisory Council on Education in Scotland, HMSO 1947

3 See the Report of the Education Committee of the Scottish Secondary Teachers' Association on Examinations, October 1969

4 *Scottish Education Department, Report on Junior Secondary Education*, HMSO, 1955

5 *Scottish Education Department (1959) Report of the Working Party on the Curriculum of the Senior Secondary School*, HMSO

6 *Secondary School Examinations other than the GCE*: a report of a Committee appointed by the Secondary Schools Examinations Council, HMSO, 1960

7 See for example: *Examining at 16: A Report of the Joint GCE/CSE Committee of the Schools Council* 1966; *A Common System of Examining at 16* Schools Council Examination Bulletin 23, Evans Methuen 1971; and *A Review of Comments on Examination Bulletin 23* Schools Council pamphlet 12, 1973

8 Wilson, J. (1976) *Examinations in Scotland: 1960–75* unpublished paper, Moray House College of Education

9 Some GCE boards are now offering Mode III options too but their scope is very limited compared to that of the CSE boards

10 *Pupils in Profile* (the report of the project). Hodder & Stoughton 1977 (p. ix)

11 Mansell, J. *Academic Profiles* Education & Training, Vol. 14 No. 9, October 1972

12 These criteria are available in the *SCRE Profile Assessment System Manual* available from SCRE, 16 Moray Place, Edinburgh, price 50p.

13 Ibid. The idea of diagnostic achievement is further explored in Harry Black's paper in the volume *The Continuous Component* which is based on the research project which grew out of the Pupil Profile development study.

14 See for example Hope, K. *Merit, Advantage and Deprivation in Scotland*, unpublished manuscript 1976

15 The research report *Pupils in Profile* demonstrates the acceptability of this procedure since teachers tended to come to a consensus in their independent assessment of basic skills: pp. 118–122

16 *Pupils in Profile*. See note 10 above.

17 For a discussion of this issue see Broadfoot, P. *Assessment, Schools & Society*, Methuen 1979

18 Broadfoot, P., 1977 *The Affective Role of Assessment – a study of pupils' involvement in the assessment process* M. Ed. Thesis, University of Edinburgh, unpublished

The Pupil Profiles research project was funded by grants from the Scottish Council for Research in Education and the Scottish Education Department. However, the views expressed are the author's own and do not necessarily reflect those of the funding bodies.

All material pertaining to the SCRE Profile Assessment System is copyright and cannot be reproduced without permission.

The financial support of the Scottish Education Department for the SCRE Pupil Profiles project is gratefully acknowledged.

7 Developments in Europe

GUY NEAVE

An overview of some European perspectives

So far, this collection has tackled the problem of providing alternative statements about the competences, skills, interests, abilities and inclinations of young people on two levels: first, on the level of individual schools; second, on the level of individual subjects. During the pioneering phase, such an approach is necessary and, indeed, perhaps the only realistic one given the particular circumstances of educational administration and division in the British Isles.

Britain is, of course, an island. Geographically, that is an undisputed fact. More disputable by far is the insidious belief which follows from this: namely that its circumstances are unique. In some cases, this is true. In the case of alternative statements for 16 year olds, it is not. In several European countries, initiatives are already forthcoming – and in some countries, already realised – in this very field. Outstanding in this regard are Denmark, France, Norway and Sweden. In these countries, however, the issue of alternative statements is somewhat more advanced than in Britain. So far, in Britain, the question has been confined to the *micro* level, to enthusiasts, teachers and thoughtful school staff. In the four countries which form the object of inquiry in this chapter, the reform is seen at the *macro* level – that is, whether it shall be introduced through the school system in general.

In this chapter, I shall look at some of the differences between educational administration and its accompanying 'ideology' in Britain and in Europe. In Europe, national education systems imply a national curriculum and thus nationally ascribed objectives. This has considerable bearing upon the whole question of national assessment norms. It also has considerable implications for the principle that subtends the whole notion of 'alternative statements' – to wit, 'democratising' assessment procedures. Now 'democratisation' is a wonderfully ambiguous term. It may be one man's meat, but it can equally be another's *poisson*. As far as assessment procedures are concerned, it contains three elements. The quantitative aspect – how many pupils are 'assessable'? Its qualitative aspect – what is to be included in the pupil profile? And, finally, its human rights aspect – do students have the right to supplement information placed on their record sheet?

On the basis of these three criteria, developments in Denmark, France, Norway and Sweden are examined. The chapter concludes that individualised pupil profiles are by no means as utopian an adventure as a worm's eye British view would suggest.

Four stages of development

It is not coincidental that those countries where assessment at 16 plus is under critical appraisal happen also to be those where the education system has moved over – or is in process of moving over – to a single type of school for a stipulated age range. European experience suggests there is a law of educational development in which assessment for all constitutes a fourth stage in what might be termed 'the universalisation' of extended secondary education.

The first stage involves structural reorganisation – that is, the merging of school types hitherto kept parallel, to form a single unit. In England and Wales, this entailed the merging of Secondary Modern and Grammar Schools to form a comprehensive school. The second stage comes with the abolition of internal tracks or streams as part of the internal reorganisation of the school. The third stage emerges with the setting up of a common core of subjects for all pupils and its progressive extension up to the end of compulsory education. The fourth stage – upon which I will concentrate in this chapter – is that of reforming assessment procedures.

These four stages may be seen as conceptually and qualitatively distinct. This is not to say, however, that other countries have necessarily worked their way through them in the same manner. Some, such as Sweden, tackled changes in external structures, classroom reorganisation and renovation of the curriculum simultaneously. Others, for instance France, devoted a first phase to changing the external structures of the education system and then waited a considerable time before embarking on the reform of the remaining three stages. Secondary reorganisation began in 1963 in France. But it was only in 1975 that the Haby reforms – so named after the then Minister of Education, René Haby – undertook to alter classroom organisation, curriculum and pupil assessment.

The British system seen from Europe

Before we go into detail about the changes in assessment procedures in the four countries we have selected, it is important to note just how exceptional the English and Welsh education systems appear from abroad, though not perhaps the Scottish. Nothing is more bizarre than that which we take for granted. And many have been the works, humorous and serious, that Europeans have devoted to understanding the English. Best known to the French is Major Thompson, an archetypal character created by Pierre Daninos. As M. Pochet, Thompson's close friend, remarked sadly on arriving at Waterloo, the English are indeed a strange race. They name their railway stations after military defeats! To confuse a filthy memorial to a great victory with a glorious reminder of a national indignity is hardly pardonable. But it illustrates the principle that what is seen as perfectly routine hides, in effect, something very exceptional when regarded from a different standpoint.

Nowhere are the differences between the English and the European perspectives greater than in the area of curriculum control. Irrespective of whether education is administered on a decentralised basis – as in the case of West Germany – or on a centralised basis – as in France or Sweden – it would generally be taken for granted that the government has the right to intervene and define the curriculum.

The government, it is argued, is a national and elected body. It has the moral responsibility for the education of its citizens. To place curricular control in the hands of teachers is, effectively, to place it in the hands of a corporation accountable to no one, at best, or acting in defence of sectional interests, at worst. In Europe, the school has, very consciously, been seen as an instrument for the development of the nation's cultural identity and as a vehicle to ensure participation in that culture. The English 'ideology' is little known but it would be seen as anarchic rather than liberal.* By some educational pundits the state has been looked upon not as a vehicle for social progress, but rather as a monstrous entity to be resisted at all costs. If one seeks the origins of this attitude, in the educational field at least, it is to be found in the battles of the late nineteenth century between the Nonconformist Radicals and supporters of the Church of England for control over schools. The one thing both Nonconformists and Churchmen held in common, apart from an unchristian dislike of one another, was their overwhelming suspicion of the state. The result has been that education, created on a municipal basis and diverse in its forms, is imbued with what may only be described as an ideological paranoia against anything that may involve the extension of the state into that domain. Corporative interests fuse in an apparent defence of municipal democracy.

---

* In the term 'English' I do not here include the Scottish ideology which is completely different and more concerned with the concept of a national culture underpinned by its education system. See Guy Neave, 'The Development of Scottish Education', *Comparative Education*, Vol. 12, No. 2, June 1976; Guy Neave and Henry Cowper, 'Less reported systems of Higher Education: Scotland', *European Journal of Education*, Feb. 1979.

In Europe, conservative and socialist parties can be identified which have no disagreement over the concept of a national curriculum. National education systems imply nationally ascribed objectives and a high degree of curricular definition if national norms are to be maintained. If they cannot be upheld, what replaces them is local arbitrariness. In this perspective, it is the role of the central state to protect its citizens and their children against the rapacity of local elites by ensuring uniform provision, practice and resources, all laid down within a clearly defined legal framework.

The differences in outlook between the English and the European have wide-ranging implications both for the role of the teacher and for the legitimacy of systems of assessment. In the introduction to this collection of essays, Adams and Burgess distinguish between three levels of responsibility for curricular development. The first of these involved teachers and pupils working for externally set syllabuses; the second entailed teachers assuming the responsibility for curriculum design themselves; and at the third, the relationship of pupil and teacher 'is one in which each helps the youngster to make something of his own life'.[1] In the four countries included in this chapter, all teachers work towards externally defined subjects. But, in contrast to England and Wales, this is not defined by examination boards under the heel of the universities. They work to syllabuses defined from the National Ministry of Education and, in the case where external examinations are still adhered to at 16 – in France and Denmark – to an examination drawn up also by the Ministry of Education.

Seen from the European angle, there is an important distinction to be made between working towards external syllabuses nationally defined, uniform in content and in the examination at the end; and working toward external syllabuses recognised as having equivalence in the national context. The former might be termed the European model and the latter the English model. In short, continental experience would suggest a fourth category should be added to the three outlined by Adams and Burgess.

Furthermore, individualisation of the curriculum to take into account the particular attributes, capacities and abilities of the pupil – the third level proposed by Adams and Burgess – is perfectly realisable within such a national framework without passing inevitably through the intermediary stage of teacher control over the curriculum. But to reach this stage requires administrative coordination from the centre. Indeed, in France, it is argued that individualisation demands a decrease in the number of pupils per class. The French reckon this should be no more than 26. Currently, around 80 per cent of French middle schools have classes at this threshold or under it. The second relates to assessment:

effort must be invested in keeping track of the individual's development, achievement and performance in a manner more coherent than before.

The English ideology of the curriculum allied to a highly diverse structure of examination boards would pose a particular obstacle to the development of pupil profiles. Public examinations having a national equivalence are, obviously, not the same thing as assessment of individual pupils. To begin with, they involve rank ordering of individuals on the basis of their nationally assessable performance at a particular moment. And the absence of a national record card system means there is no supplemental information recognised as nationally valid for those who, through quirks of administrative myopia and arbitrariness, are regarded as incapable of public assessment. Pupils who stand in need of a credible and nationally valid system to monitor and record the development of their aptitudes over time are thus uncatered for. There is no system of pupil profiles as yet accepted as nationally valid, though certain initiatives outlined earlier in this book show the difficulties of the pioneers in the field in getting their initiatives accepted even by local industry and commerce. Yet, even the latest foray into developing a common examination for all at 16 plus clings to the unacceptable fiction that 40 per cent of 16 year olds are so inept that they cannot be admitted to public examination. As a rethink of an old problem it is, by all European standards, risible, though as a historical document it serves to reflect that long tradition of official pessimism about the educability of young people in England and Wales.[2] Like the Bourbons of the post Napoleonic Restoration, officialdom appears to have learnt nothing and forgotten as much.

Even European countries that retain a public examination for 16 year olds – for instance the *Brevet d'Etudes de Premier Cycle* in France – have a back-up system in the form of school record cards. In France, for example, this comes in the shape of the *livret scolaire*. If this appears as overcomplicated on the principle that to have both belt and braces is to indulge in sartorial redundancy, it is at least comforting for those who will in any case be denied the braces of public examinations still to have the belt of the record card to preserve them from 'going forth naked into the world'.

From a European standpoint, the various proposals and initiatives outlined in this collection are really a non-issue. In short, national pupil profiles are not utopian. They are already in many countries, Sweden, Norway and France, a practical reality. Indeed, amongst the Scandinavian countries a clear tendency appears to be emerging in which record cards are themselves becoming a substitute for the once-off national examination system. We will go into the details of this later.

To sum up this section, we can now present a typology of countries according to whether the importance is laid either on examinations or on pupil profiles. In the first category is the traditional reliance on public examinations alone. We find here the United Kingdom and Denmark. In the second fall countries in a stage of transition in which public examinations still exist as the major instrument for national assessment though with an alternative source of information contained in the pupil's individual record card, calibrated to national norms. Into this category would fall France. And, finally, we have those countries where the major instrument stating the attainment of both 16 and 18 year olds is the pupil profile system, nationally standardised, in which the examination has given place to a regular series of standardised tests routinely administered to all children at certain points in their school careers. In this group fall Norway and Sweden.

A second development, of no lesser relevance to the question of assessment for all, is the number of public examinations young people are required to sit during the course of their school careers. The tendency over the past few years in England and Wales (quite apart from Scotland) has, on paper at least, been to increase this. The apotheosis of this development is to be seen in Scotland where the able 18 year old has, like as not, sat O Grade, the Higher Grade and the Certificate of Sixth Year Studies. In many European countries, of which France is one example and West Germany another, the tendency is towards sitting one national examination, usually corresponding to the level at which the pupil will leave the education system. Among the Scandinavian countries the trend appears to be towards decreasing the number of occasions when formal marks are given.[3]

Developments in the area of alternative assessment in Europe

Before going into the details of how systems of national pupil profiles work in the various European countries selected for this paper, it is necessary to clarify some of the basic tenets that have been advanced in justification of such devices. It is held, for instance, that individual pupil profiles are 'democratic'. But 'democracy', like that other bugaboo of educational misunderstanding, 'standards', is capable of numerous conflicting interpretations. Taken within the context of alternative outcomes for 16 year olds, the democratic principle can be said to consist of three elements: first, the quantitative aspect of democratisation – that all school pupils are involved in the system. The second is the qualitative aspect – what should be included so that as accurate a picture of the individual pupil as possible may be provided? And, third, the individual rights aspect of democratisation – can students themselves supplement the information placed on record?

In those European countries where 100 per cent national record cards for pupils exist, they are democratic on the basis of the first criterion. It should be pointed out in the British context, however, that to give record cards to some whilst relying on public examinations as a statement of the aptitudes of others is not. Even to limit record cards for 100 per cent of pupils in one particular sector of the education system, let us say, the state sector, and to exempt the private sector on the grounds that examinations are more suited to its denizens, violates this same principle. In both instances, it is merely an admission of the arbitrary nature of public examinations by excluding between 30 and 40 per cent of the age range in the former case and between 5 and 6 per cent in the latter.

Furthermore, it is doubtful whether pupil profile systems, based on myriad local schemes, each gathering information on different items, could be said to be 'democratic' on the second criterion. The qualitative aspect of democracy, it is said, implies a strong national frame and an agreement on a wide range of common items in the dossiers of all pupils.

In the next section, we look at developments in alternative forms of assessment in four countries where the system of individual profiles is already well established: Denmark, France, Norway and Sweden. In these countries the debate centres on the qualitative and individual rights aspects of the issue. By taking the four countries in this order we hope to be able to show the development of the problem along a species of conceptual continuum ranging from Denmark where, despite proposals of a radical nature, examinations still retain their traditional form, through to Sweden where pupil profile systems have been in operation from 1963.

1   Denmark: examination reform – abolition of examinations later?

In Denmark, compulsory education is provided in the nine year comprehensive school, the Folkeskole, which covers the age range 7 to 16, though pupils have the right to a tenth year according to the Public Schools (Free) Act of 1975.[4] Though talk of reforming the examination system has been rife for a number of years, only in the spring of 1978 was a new examination system introduced in Denmark. In future, assessment will be based on separate sets of marks. Beginning in the 8th Grade (15 plus) marks will be awarded for proficiency on the one hand and on examination results on the other.[5] Marks for proficiency will be based on the level of the course content – whether basic or advanced – and show the individual's position compared to his or her classmates. By contrast, examination marks will be used to assess how far the pupil has met the objectives and level of knowledge laid down by the Ministry of Education in a stipulated subject. The aim of this innovation is to set up a marking system that is nationally comparable. Previously this was not the case, since examinations corresponded to the level at which pupils were taught – either basic or advanced. Henceforth written examinations are to be aligned on the basic course in all subjects.

In many respects, this somewhat traditional structure may be seen as a compromise between the political parties – Social Democrats on the one hand and Liberals on the other. In 1975, for example, the Social Democrats proposed that the examinations be replaced by a school leaving certificate which confined itself to listing the subjects studied by the pupil. Political realities decreed otherwise. In order to get the reform of the Folkeskole through Parliament, the Social Democrats needed the support of the Liberals, who had declared in favour of retaining examinations.[6] The current situation is that pupils may sit for a qualifying certificate in Mathematics, English, German and Physics/ Chemistry at the end of the ninth year (16 plus). Though grades are awarded, no particular grade is required for a pass.[7] At the end of the tenth year, pupils may sit for the School Leaving Certificate (*Folkskolens afgangsprove*) either in the same subject or in a broader range if they so wish.[8] Those leaving school at the end of year seven receive a written report of their capacities and aptitudes.

How far this structure will survive and for how long is a matter for conjecture. At the present moment, the Danes are engaged in a long-term review of the whole education system with the aim of drawing up an overall planning framework for the next fifteen years. The group entrusted with this task, the U90 Commission (*Education 1990*), has identified three major priorities: greater emphasis on equality; new aims associated with the socialisation of young people; and, finally, changes in the type of qualification that is likely to be required between now and the end of the century.[9] Obviously, all three priority areas have some bearing upon forms of assessment. We will concentrate, however, upon proposals for changing the qualification requirements since it is here that implications for assessment procedures are the most immediate.

The basic proposition of the U90 outline is that the individual, to an increasing extent, needs qualifications to enable him to take part in the life of the community. From this premise flow a number of consequences: first, irrespective of the future mode of assessment, it will have to give adequate recognition of the overall activities of the individual. These, the outline states, fall into four clear headings – family life, leisure, working life and social life. Second, assessment should have less to do with activities *in school* than with preparing the young person to lead his life in these four areas. Third, changes in the concept of society will inevitably bring about changes in what are deemed 'relevant qualifications'. At present, qualifications are determined by the traditions and structures of the labour market and by the subject 'nexus' in school. These influences are extremely narrow though they have the apparent advantage of appearing precise and measurable. Rather than relying on these forces to determine either curriculum or assessment, the U90 plan looks towards identifying general skills both relevant and desirable across all four sectors of human activity. Conceptually, this is an important development, all the more so since the economic crisis and the escalating levels of youth unemployment have, more implicitly than by design, tended to couch the problem of alternative assessment within the traditional and linear flow from school to work.[10] Amongst the general skills so far specified are precision in carrying out one's work, a methodological approach to problems and an ability to adapt.[11]

2   France: the reform of the French education system, its objectives and the role of the computerised pupil profile system

The Haby reform of 1976 involved a root and branch restructuring of the whole of the French education system from the pre-primary school to the upper secondary school. It is a vast undertaking and will only reach completion around 1981–2. This being so, we will make reference here only to the principal objectives attributed to primary and lower secondary education and to their influence upon the question of assessment. Outstanding amongst the features to emerge from this reform is the notion that education systems should be planned *in toto*. Thus the objectives ascribed to primary schools, for example, may be coordinated with those assigned to secondary education. The prime objective was, then, to ensure better physical as well as pedagogic links across the two administratively separate sectors. The second objective of the Haby reform was to redefine the curriculum to take full cognisance of what John Raven so eloquently terms 'the ability to make human beings human'.[12]

The task of the primary school is to promote (*favoriser*) the development of the child in its total aspect as a growing human being (*un être humain en devenir*). All possible care should be taken to husband the whole range of options and avenues that will, later, contribute to the individual's self-realisation (*épanouissement*). And equal attention should be paid in seeking out, the better to prevent, those various handicaps which may compromise a child's development.[13]

Amongst the objectives attributed to the comprehensive middle school or college is the purveyance of the fundamental elements of a modern and general culture regarded as indispensable if each young French boy and girl is to play his or her part as an adult citizen. It should also permit the continuation of further study either in permanent education or in the upper secondary school. Notable amongst the goals set aside for compulsory secondary education is the development of the affective domain just as much as the cognitive. The middle school, the Ministry Circular continues, must allow the pupil to discover his tastes and aptitudes, thereby preparing him for the important decisions he will have to make at the end of compulsory education.[14]

With the national curriculum now specified in terms of operational objectives, it was apparent that the old *livret scolaire* – a personal dossier that accompanied a pupil throughout his school career, usually containing his subject marks – was no longer sufficient. Accordingly, M. Haby introduced the computerised pupil record card system in 1977. The aim of the new profile was to take into account what has been termed elsewhere 'a multiple ability concept of talent'.[15] Like the *livret* the new computerised pupil record card was to accompany each pupil right through the education system, from pre-primary to upper secondary school. The items on which it was based were wide-ranging and, in many cases, highly sensitive: school results, whether the pupils attained the objectives stipulated both for his age range and in the subject area. This is routine. In addition to this species of information were to be allied others on matters such as family background, the condition of the family, the child's medical history, psychological comportment, behaviour in class as well as behaviour with fellows. In the affective domain were included such items as 'sense of responsibility', 'team spirit' 'willingness to work with others'.

To place information about family background and the non-confidential details of a pupil's medical history on the same file as his school record was perhaps indelicate. But Ministry officials justified this on the grounds that it was extremely important to identify those children whose background suggested they were 'at risk'. Only in this way could the resources of an adequate programme of compensatory education be marshalled in time. The other role of the computerised pupil profile was to ensure that the orientation stage – the first two years of middle school – was based on long-term information, most of which could only be gathered during the pupil's passage through primary school. Guidance was to be based on hard and objective data, and not just on the personal impressions of the guidance counsellor.

This new version of the pupil profile system was not destined simply for schools alone. It was also to follow the pupil if he left at 16 to enter an apprenticeship training scheme (*centre de formation d'apprentis*).[16] In short, it was also to be a vehicle of information crossing the line between school and work.

As far as our three criteria of 'democratisation' are concerned, M. Haby's computerised pupil profile system fulfilled the first. It was to be distributed amongst 100 per cent of the school population. It also obeyed the second criterion – namely, the items included, both in the affective and in the cognitive domain, were nationally standardised. Where it fell down was in the area of individual rights. Only part of the information contained in it was to be available to parents. This concerned behaviour, attainment and achievement. But the dossier in full was available only to teachers and school administrators. Parts of it, then, were of a confidential nature, though, as a legal safeguard, parents, guardians and pupils, if they were of the age of majority, could demand to see the whole dossier.

The objections to the new pupil profile system
One of the major objections to the enterprise was precisely its computerised nature. As one well-known weekly put it, 'The fate of the kids with rickets is improved not one iota simply by counting the number of kids with rickets: what is needed is better living conditions, less unemployment and less anxiety. Do you really need social surveys to discover that? Haby's proposals are little more than an imbecility and his indicators are too magnificently vague.'[17]

Faced with a growing uproar, M. Haby backtracked. In February 1978, just before the general elections, he threw the child to the wolves. 'I have not the slightest intention of laying my head on the block for the sake of the computerised record card system', he announced. Two months later, his successor, M. Christian Beullac, abolished it. M. Beullac's generosity was greeted with roars of approval and jubilation. And the wolves of the education world now had the head of M. Haby as well as his brainchild to gnaw upon and play with.

In fact, M. Haby vanished not because of an objection to the record card system as a matter of principle. That had long been accepted with the *livret scolaire*. Though the issue fell into the arena of educational policy, a totally different principle was involved, namely that of confidentiality and individual rights. And this principle is not limited simply to a centralised education system, nor is it any the less acute for having education based on the principle of decentralisation of powers. This for two simple reasons: first, computers make nonsense of constitutional arrangements and administrative niceties – or rather, they allow people to set them at nought; and second, because the issue of confidentiality and individual rights is as delicate in centralised as in regionally controlled or municipally run systems of education. And here, it should be noted that, despite the centralised nature of French education, the French public, parents and teachers, were still powerful enough to have the system rescinded when it did appear to infringe the bounds of confidentiality. What one sees here is a conflict between one of our criteria of 'democracy' when applied to assessment procedures setting at nought the other two. The dilemma thus posed is not only one of principle in the abstract. It also involves questions of practicality. How can education systems fulfil a policy of equality if the information needed to implement it in, let us say, the area of compensatory education, requires the routine gathering of information that is often highly sensitive? It is not sufficient to argue that teachers can be trusted to be like the cat, discreet. The same confidence applied to the individual invalidates the lack of confidence when applied to many individuals, namely, government services. Nor is it sufficient to see a guarantee of individual rights simply by conferring on schools the right to create, *comme bon leur semble*, their own individual assessment systems. For that, in effect, would appear to go contrary to the quantitative and the qualitative aspects involved in democratising assessment.

3   Norway: recognition of the benefits of 'informal evaluation'

Early in 1978, the Norwegian Committee on Evaluation made its report. It recommended that as a form of assessment, marks should be abolished in the 7 to 16 comprehensive school. Instead, more weight should be placed upon informal methods of assessment. The Committee believes that informal approaches are a significant way of enhancing the motivation of pupils. Several research enquiries undertaken on behalf of the commission appear to underwrite this claim.[18] By contrast, as a means of assessing the pre-16 age groups, marks have unduly restrictive influences in several areas. First, they limit the freedom of subject choice. Pupils are apt to choose those subjects which afford the most marks and this introduces an in-built bias towards the cognitive subjects, it is said. Second, attempts to develop alternative methods of working, for example, either individual enquiry or projects carried out by a team of pupils, suffer from the sense of competition marks engender. Third, the use of marks as a basis of assessment encourages both teachers and pupils to place overweening importance on that part of school activity which is amenable to measurement.

With ideas similar to the Danish proposals contained in the outline stage of the U90 Commission, the Norwegians feel that assessment ought to take into account all the activities in school and not merely the work undertaken by pupils. Similar, too, are the suggestions that assessment for the 16 year olds and under should recognise in future the significance of the non-cognitive area in the individual's development. However, the logic of the Norwegian argument takes them far beyond the boundaries imposed either by the French or the Danes. Assessment of pupil progress, the Norwegian Committee pointed out, is only one aspect of the overall evaluation of both institutions and the education system. It should also be linked to the evaluation of institutional performance. By associating the two, assessment of the individual with evaluation of the institution itself, it is possible, the Committee reckoned, to ascertain how far the school's overall activities have reached the general goals ascribed to it. The same exercise would also enable both pupils and teachers to judge whether resources allocated to the individual school, be they time budgeting, staff or equipment, were being used in the most efficacious way.

The concept is particularly interesting since it assumes that pupil assessment represents the *micro* level of evaluation which, quite logically, may be extended to the *macro* level of assessing those institutions in which the development of individuals takes place. In many respects, the Norwegian suggestions bear a certain similarity with some of the more controversial aims associated with M. Haby's computerised pupil profile. One of these was to use the French data system as the basis for a primary planning instrument at national level, monitoring the performance of the education system at all levels, from municipality to region and finally to the country as a whole. But, whereas M. Haby's computerised instrument served to reinforce control from above, it would seem that the Norwegian proposal, by involving both pupils and teachers in the evaluation of their school, seeks to reinforce control from the base. This leads us to the general proposition that the controversy over new forms of assessment is not that, intrinsically, they imply greater centralisation in control. They can indeed be used to that end. But the very possibility that they can be used for both purposes simultaneously, depending on which areas of the education system are allocated to central government and which to the municipality or to parents and teachers, means that the monolithic concept of the education system as *either* centralised *or* de-centralised and that democratic control depends either on one or on the other, is no longer tenable.

The Norwegian proposal for institutional evaluation by pupils and teachers also has its educational aspects. It is thought to enhance the involvement of pupils in the daily running and routine of their school and thus may be seen as a powerful catalyst for the improvement of motivation. It is a suggestion well worth close attention from British educationists and administrators since it holds out the possibility of breaking through that 'stultifying environment' which, all too often, surrounds educational establishments.[19]

4   Sweden: towards the abolition of marks as a form of assessment?

The system of pupil record cards has been in operation since 1962 in Sweden. However, amongst the most recent developments has been the publication in 1977 of the recommendations of the Commission on Marking, set up in 1973. Like the Norwegians, it recommended the abolition of marks as a form of assessment for the 7 to 16 comprehensive school. But, whilst the Norwegians came down in favour of retaining marks for the upper school, the Swedes have devised a complicated system of points for passage to the *gymnasialskola*, the 16 to 18 upper school. The Commission has recommended that pupils should receive a certificate on leaving the 7 to 16 school which would state what the pupil has studied and the level reached.[20] Assessment as such will not disappear, but will, it is suggested, take place at the end of each term at a meeting of parents, teachers and pupils. Other matters, such as pupil's welfare and behaviour, would be discussed at the same time. Though a majority recommendation, this idea has not gained the support of members identified with the Conservative–Liberal coalition. They remain in favour of retaining marks during the last three years of the 7 to 16 comprehensive school.

The current system of assessment in Swedish comprehensive schools is based upon a five point scale, five being the highest and one the lowest. The categories of pass/fail are no longer used.[21] To ensure overall comparability, the National Board of Education provides standardised tests each year in the majority of school subjects. These are of two kinds, diagnostic and achievement. Though voluntary, around 90 to 95 per cent of pupils sit the achievement tests each year.[22] Testing takes place once a year in 3rd Grade (9 years of age), 6th Grade (12 years of age) and 7th Grade (13 plus). In the 8th and 9th Grades this is increased to twice a year.[23] The purpose of testing is to establish the position of the particular class in relation to all others at a similar level throughout the country. They are, then, the basis of drawing up national norms. Though providing the framework of national standardisation, they are not used to crosscheck whether the pupil has been assigned the 'right mark' on the five point scale.[24]

The five point scale itself is a 'relative marking system' – that is, it shows the position of the individual pupil relative to others at the same level throughout the land. Distribution follows a normal curve: 14 per cent of the school population fall into grade 1 or grade 5, 48 per cent into grades 2 and 4 with the remaining 38 per cent into grade 3. Though assessment is criteria- and skill-referenced, teachers still have considerable latitude in assigning marks.

The development of standardised achievement tests was one of the major thrusts of the innovation programmes of the 1950s and 1960s. Their extension has meant that neither the comprehensive school nor the *gymnasialskola* is subject to external examinations. Recently, two new trends have emerged. The first of these is the development of diagnostic assessment tests as part of remedial education. Though diagnostic tests can indicate where and how pupils fail, only rarely do they suggest courses for action. Over the past seven or eight years considerable effort has gone into finding ways around this *lacuna*. The second development is towards evaluation based on the non-cognitive domain which, as we have seen, has gained considerable impetus with the recommendations of the Commission on Marking. The National Board of Education's test development section has set aside considerable resources for the evaluation of non-cognitive functions upon teaching and learning. Amongst the areas under attention are the social development of the individual, his emotional maturation as well as his physical and manual development.

Conclusion

In this chapter, I have considered some of the recent developments in assessment at 16 in four countries: France, Denmark, Norway and Sweden. Against this background, the United Kingdom appears exceptional for a number of reasons. First, whereas all the countries under consideration have a 100 per cent national system of assessment, some assured by examinations – for instance, Denmark – others both by national examination and record card profiles – for instance, France – or simply by standardised test results entered on record cards – for instance, Sweden – the United Kingdom possesses merely a partial system or rather series of partial systems having national equivalence. Second, in none of the countries considered was the instrument for stating the achievements, performance, ambitions, sociability and behaviour of young people so incomplete as in Britain. Not all young people in France for example will sit national examinations. But those who do not are not denied a nationally recognised instrument to show what they have been able to do.

A further characteristic common to all four countries was the acceptance of what has been termed earlier 'a multiple ability concept of talent'. The Danish case illustrated very nicely the justification of this development. In part, it was empirical. Industrial and social change – and unemployment should perhaps be regarded under this general rubric – make the forecasting of particular skill requirements especially difficult. With the development of permanent education, the possibility of acquiring job-specific skills, it might be argued, can be left until later. What appears to be needed at the present time is a development of broadly general skills, applicable over wide areas of the individual's existence. The same conclusion was reached in France, though departing from slightly different premises. Planners from the Ministry of Education justify the introduction of a common core course in the comprehensive middle school on the grounds that it is easier to retain an individual having a solid basis of general skills – meticulousness, persistence in tasks set, etc. – than to retrain the same person whose basic education rests upon specific skills and techniques aimed at employment in a narrow and specific sector of the economy.[25]

This raises the important question of what should be included in pupil profiles: in other words, the second of our criteria of 'democratising' assessment procedures. The multiple concept of talent requires a far closer liaison between the education system *proprement dit* and representatives from other institutions in which the individual will work, live and have his being, than has hitherto been the case in the United Kingdom. Here, it is reasonable to suggest that what does go into the dossiers is too important simply to be the unique responsibility of the teaching profession. War, as Clemenceau observed, is too important to be left to generals.

Here again, the French and certainly the Swedish experience may be of particular interest. In both cases, the drawing up of a core curriculum was not an enterprise carried out within the confines of the Ministry of Education or the National Board of Education. It involved also the sustained cooperation at central government level of both trades unions and employers in order to ascertain what might be considered the key and basic skills that young people ought to have on leaving school. In this area it is the Swedes, however, who have developed this approach to its fullest extent. As part of the curriculum development for the introduction of the comprehensive school 7 to 16, a number of research undertakings were launched to ascertain how far the skills nurtured in school were actively employed at work. The results were astounding. Around 10 per cent of the knowledge purveyed in school was used later at the workplace. Or, put another way, 90 per cent was not. The conclusion the Swedes reached was that the curriculum should be designed in the light of the types of skills actively utilised in earning one's living; and that the curriculum should have the overall aim of raising the level of utilisable skills.

The implications of this are far-ranging, not merely in the patterns of partnership necessary to reformulate the curriculum in the light of skills acknowledged as nationally desirable or humanly necessary. There are also implications for the concept of the curriculum itself. For if skills are to become the constant, the basis on which pupils are assessed, rather than 'subjects', then one might suggest that the curriculum and the content assume all the trappings of a variable. This has already been acknowledged in certain quarters. Hence, neither the curriculum nor its content can be regarded *sub speciae aeternitatis*. And in this connection, there is a commission currently at work in Sweden with the remit to determine how, in the light of changes in the labour market, and in the light of changes in attitudes of young people towards it, the curriculum may be updated, the better to foster the general skills now deemed important.

This is not to say that the decision as to which items ought to figure on a pupil's dossier should rest entirely with central government in partnership with representatives from the various economic sectors to which pupils will ultimately go. But, if European experience is anything to go by, it does at least suggest that decisions as to the 'frame items' – those forming the national profile as opposed to the individual profile, the former being coterminous with the cognitive domain broadly speaking and the latter with the affective – presupposes rather less segmentation between educational and other institutions than has hitherto been the case.

Interesting though it might be, prescription ought to occupy only a small place in this conclusion.

Finally, we come to the question of examinations. In three of the four countries included in this paper, a clear trend against external examinations at the 16 plus stage appears to be emerging. In Sweden, they have been abolished. Norway proposes to abolish them and Denmark lives in the hope they may be abolished in the future. Thus, in those countries commonly regarded as being in the forefront of educational development, examinations at 16 plus as the major method of assessment are by no means looked upon as inevitable, ineluctable or immovable. Rather the contrary. Limited in the information they purvey, restrictive of pupil choice, examinations appear very much like the salt that lost his savour – 'fit only to be trodden under the foot of man'.

References

1 See page 10 above.
2 Cmnd 7281, *School Examinations: Report of the steering committee established to consider proposals for replacing the General Certificate of Education Ordinary level and Certificate of Secondary Education examinations by a common system of examining (Waddell Report)*, London, 1978, HMSO
3 Osnes, J., *Grunnskolen in Norden*, Copenhagen, 1977, the Nordic Council
4 *The Danish Education System*, Copenhagen, 1977, Ministry of Education, (mimeo), p. 1
5 *Denmark: a new marking and examination system in the final year of comprehensive schooling*, Council of Europe Newsletter 1/78, pp. 7–8
6 *Denmark: Folkeskole reform bill at least enacted*, Council of Europe Newsletter 2/75, p. 12
7 *The Danish Education System* op. cit., p. 4
8 See note 6 above
9 *Central Council for Education, Interim Outline of the U90 Plan*, Copenhagen, March 1977

10 On this issue see Guy Neave (ed.), *Research Perspectives on the Transition from School to Work*, Amsterdam/Lisse, Swets & Zeitlinger, 1977

11 See note 9 above

12 See Raven's contribution to this collection, page 104

13 *Objectifs par niveaux d'enseignement* Council of Europe Newsletter 3/76, p. 6

14 *ibid.*, p. 8

15 See Raven page 106

16 *Bulletin Officiel de l'Education Nationale no. 30*, 1 September 1977

17 Thomas, Bernard, *Fichiers en tout genre: tous des flics*, Le Canard Enchaîné, August 31st 1977

18 *Norway: assessment at school*, Council of Europe Newsletter 1/78, p. 20

19 See Raven page 104

20 *Sweden: proposals for the modification of school assessment procedures*, Council of Europe Newsletter 2/77, p. 35

21 Orring, J., *School in Sweden*, Stockholm 1969

22 *National Board of Education, Testing and evaluation in Swedish schools*, Stockholm, 1970, Bureau L4

23 *ibid.*

24 Hermansson, Hartwig, *Upper secondary school reform in Sweden: micro level approach*, Vereniging de Samenwerkende Landelijke Pedagogische Centre, Netherlands, 25 January, 1977 (mimeo) pp. 10–12

25 See Neave, *Editorial introduction, Research perspectives on the transition*, op. cit. (note 10 above)

8 The forms and functions of assessment

HARRY BLACK

Everyone is an educational expert. Having spent many of his formative years in school it is hardly surprising that everyone knows what is meant by examinations and assessment. Indeed, there is a powerful logic which says that the whole concept of testing is fair. We all know the exception, the millionaire without a single O level to his name, but by and large it seems just that those who display the greatest success at the hurdle of the external examinations end up with the better jobs – it seems inevitable since they have shown that they are more able.

The logic of assessment

Commonsense expertise of course tends to have problems. Research findings in many countries including Britain have suggested that terminal examinations both at school and university are poor predictors of future academic success. Ingenkamp,[1] for example, in a survey of twenty-six studies in German-speaking countries of the relationship between school leaving marks and academic success found correlation coefficients of between 0.06 and 0.49 with a mean amongst the studies of 0.29. Similar studies in Britain including those of Petch (1961),[2] Barnett and Lewis (1963),[3] Entwistle *et al.* (1971)[4] and Powell (1975),[5] have shown comparable results. If academic marks have such poor predictive validity for future success in academic life, there can be little optimism as to their value for non-academic prognostication.

The commonsense meaning of 'more able' is also somewhat ambiguous. The employer who asks for five CSEs or four O levels is asking for information at the 'general ability' level. With the frequent exception of English and mathematics, the actual subjects are seldom important. Students and teachers, however, see examination results as more than a reflection of general ability. Unexpected results are explained, at least in part, by the chance factor of examination content and the result is seen as the sum of marks for attainment in specific abilities. Our present examination system, however, does not appear to satisfy either requirement particularly well. If measures of general intelligence are required, examinations which purport to relate to the specific objectives of a subject are not the best way of providing them. Equally, the provision of a single subject grade can hardly hope to satisfy those who are interested in specific abilities. A profile reporting system such as that suggested in Broadfoot's paper may well be the solution.

It must therefore seem strange that examinations which have a low ability to predict future success and which provide very little real information about the specific abilities of their candidates, should so dominate school assessment. Perhaps less difficult to understand is the growing dissatisfaction amongst those who are aware of such problems and who seek an alternative to the present forms of assessment.

However, while the continuing search for an alternative solution to terminal assessment is important it is essential that the underlying meaning of 'assessment' should be examined. Assessment and certification are not synonymous. 'Assessment' subsumes many other concepts such as intelligence tests, class tests, end-of-term exams, reporting and indeed, certification. Unfortunately, in many instances, not least in the argument for or against the present form of certification, all those concepts are lumped together. The result is that many of the valid criticisms which we can make of certification and reporting as they stand are ascribed to assessment in its broader context.

The dangers in this are twofold. First, by not making the distinction we may sweep aside much of the potential of existing curriculum oriented assessment practised as good teaching in the classroom. Second, and equally important, we will not focus on the particular problems and criticisms which are associated with the other forms of assessment which can only serve to reinforce the unfortunate dominance of certification and reporting in research, development and the public eye.

Formative or summative assessment?

The distinction which I would like to make here is between assessment to satisfy the needs of society (which normally takes the form of 'summative' assessment) and assessment to help in both teaching and student learning (which is most usefully 'formative assessment'). It is the writer's view that while summative assessment may need to be changed quite radically in order that it might take account of a wider spectrum of student characteristics than students' subject-based cognitive attainment, the change required in formative assessment is more in the order of the focus on and systematisation of existing good teaching practices. But what grounds are there for my assertion that the criticisms made of summative assessment as practised do not apply to formative assessment?

First let it be made clear that we are not necessarily thinking about what at present happens, but rather, what should happen: that is, formative assessment should be an aid to teaching and student learning. Therefore, we are no longer thinking about putting our students in rank order but simply ascertaining whether or not they have succeeded in learning whatever it was that we intended that they should learn. Of course, our assessments of such phenomena can only sample this understanding, but the important thing to note is that this is different from comparing one student with the rest in rank order.

Second, it was a criticism of external examinations that they appear to be poor predictors of future success. But in formative, domain-referenced assessment we have a different definition of validity. We are no longer interested in prognostication, but rather in establishing the presence of satisfactory learning. And so the question is no longer 'what does this result tell us about the student's likely future success?', but rather, 'does the result tell us about the domain which we are sampling, or something else?'. In taking this step we have moved from the problems and pitfalls of predictive validity to a new set of problems concerning content validity. The important point to make is not that there are no problems of validity in formative assessment, but that the problems are different and require different solutions.

A third criticism of existing summative assessment was that external examinations tend to dominate the curriculum. It would be rather blinkered to suggest that by changing the form of summative assessment we would overcome this problem. It seems inevitable that both student and teacher will attend to whatever is construed as the most positive way of playing the system. Essentially, summative assessment dominates the curriculum because it is seen by both student and teacher as a hurdle. Formative assessment, however, should be seen as outside this argument. Of course, in many classrooms almost all forms of assessment are seen as hurdles and so much of their potential to contribute to student learning is lost. But if carried out properly formative assessment does not dominate the curriculum. It becomes an integral and positive element in the learning process.

Problems in formative assessment

Of course it would be wrong to conclude from this that formative assessment is without problems, but what is being suggested is that the problems and therefore the changes required are different from those which lead us to alternative forms of summative assessment. In fact, most of the criticisms which can be made of established approaches to formative assessment stem from the lack of differentiation between the two forms of assessment and the greater prominence given to the various forms of summative assessment.

What are these criticisms? No mention has yet been made of the commonly used term 'continuous assessment' because it is in the common usage of this concept that the first problem lies. If formative assessment is to give useful feedback on teaching and student learning one would assume that it is synonymous with continuous assessment. In practice this is seldom the case. Continuous assessment in most schools is seen primarily as a staccato form of summative assessment – really the end-of-term exam in small sections taken throughout the year. The feedback to individual students is normally in the form of a composite mark bringing together all the various concepts, skills and elements of knowledge in one general attainment grade. Furthermore, this assessment normally takes place at the end of a section of work when in many subjects it is too late to take remedial action. The result has been to institutionalise almost every form of classroom test into the hurdle construct which characterises summative assessment.

Another criticism is the pressure which is put on teachers to make their formative assessment conform with the school reporting system. In many schools, end-of-term grades have to be norm-referenced with a specific percentage in each grade. No matter how good or bad the teaching may have been, an assumption of failure is built into learning which has no logic other than that of the certification process which is essentially a competition. Is the teacher to set his tests with acceptable attainment so high that no matter how well the students understand the work, half of them are bound to fail? What kind of motivation is that, and what does it say of a curriculum containing objectives which 50 per cent of the class will not attain? On the other hand, can the teacher tell 90 per cent of the class that they have attained what he intended, and then 'fail' half of them in his terminal report? Teachers consequently become sceptical and regard assessment as something external to the learning process with the result that formative assessment ranks low in priority when it is really an essential teaching tool.

Again, where the construct to be taken from a test result is a comparison with the other examinees it seems logical that the utmost care be taken in ensuring both the discipline of the testing situation and the marking process: the teacher inevitably tests and marks while the student is tested and receives. The student, although central in focus, has a circumscribed and passive role to play. In formative assessment, however, the feedback is primarily for the student yet the system used in most classrooms closely resembles that of the summative test. Perhaps most undervalued is the potential of the student to assess and record his own progress, an approach which has the considerable advantages of releasing the teacher to deal with individual problems and giving the student feedback in a form which closely parallels the assessment which he continually makes of his own learning.

Diagnostic assessment

What then should be the nature of formative assessment? The Scottish Council for Research in Education has recently completed the first phase of a programme in Diagnostic Assessment. This was designed to evaluate the potential of a diagnostic approach in secondary schools and worked intensively with a group of about thirty teachers in six schools for eighteen months. What we were trying to do was not new. It was an extension of good teaching practice which as a result of the dominant and narrow perception of assessment as reporting outlined above has never really been systematised into good formative assessment.

The teachers saw diagnostic assessment in terms of three basic questions which became the outline of our model of diagnostic assessment. See Figure 8(i):

Figure 8(i)

Mode	Focus of assessment	Areas of concern	
I	The class	The success of the class in attaining the intended objective	Each of these can contribute to curriculum evaluation; e.g. are the objectives suitable, is the teaching strategy successful, etc?
II	The individual pupil	Which pupils have not attained the objective?	
III	The individual pupil	What is/are the reason(s) for the pupil not attaining the objectives?	

It would be impossible here to cover all the studies in the Diagnostic Assessment Project, and the reader who is interested in the potential and problems of diagnostic assessment as seen by the project might like to consult the report[6] in one or more of its formats. However, three case studies taken from the project might serve to highlight a few of the potential uses of diagnostic assessment in the classroom.

Case study one: continuous assessment in a modern languages department

The first is a 'before' and 'after' story. 'Before' is no criticism of the French department. Ingenkamp,[7] using illustrations from the work of Weiss in

Austria and de Groot in the Netherlands, has shown that foreign languages along with mathematics tend to be the most strictly marked in schools, and the particular school studied here had an established and well-tried policy of continuous assessment before becoming associated with the project. The question which had to be asked, however, was what was being assessed.

Figure 8(ii)

An analysis of the content of 1st year continuous assessment tests

Skill or knowledge tested	Test 1	Test 2	Test 3	Test 4	Test 5
Aural comprehension	x	x	x		x
Vocabulary recall	x	x	x		x
Background knowledge	x				x
Written comprehension		x	x	x	
Grammar recall/recognition		x	x	x	x

Figure 8(ii) above shows the teacher's own evaluation of the content of the department's first-year continuous assessment programme. His conclusion was that his testing aims were inconsistent and that many items were difficult to categorise, for example, when a student was shown a country on a blank map and asked to give its French name no clear conclusion could be drawn – did he simply not recognise that country or could he not recall its French name?

However, with the exception of background knowledge which was obviously underdeveloped, each of the skills appears to have been assessed regularly and there was a fairly uniform approach to assessment throughout the term. But two questions, which are worth asking of any teacher, gave more cause for concern. The first was to what extent tests reflected the essential aims of the course. Had they been planned to show both teacher and student their success or lack of it; or had they been created as an afterthought, largely to satisfy the needs of the reporting system? Among the reflections in this case was that oral skills which were ranked very high amongst teaching aims were not assessed at all.

The second question was what the teachers had done with the results of these tests. Superficially it appeared as if there existed a longitudinal record for each student in five areas. The teacher would know how an individual had progressed in aural comprehension and vocabulary recall because each had been tested four times. In fact this was not the case as, for recording purposes, the marks in each section had been added together to give a general mark in French. Assessment was obviously taking place but to make full use of its potential for diagnosis, the teacher had to look more closely at what should be assessed and what to do with the results.

Case study two: the assessment of affective pupil character-istics in a technical studies department.

If the first case study centred on the question of what to assess, the second, which considers the assessment of affective student characteristics in a technical studies department, addresses itself more to the question of how to assess. What to assess is of course as complex a problem in the affective domain as in the cognitive and was examined by the project more closely in another of the case studies. However, in this particular instance the choice of characteristics to be considered was the result of discussion between the teachers and the research team.

In some ways this was an example of the reporting system dictating assessment such that continuous assessment was not formative but staccato summative. The teachers were obliged by the school reporting system to complete an open-ended statement on each student each term and found it difficult to make sound comments which did not resort to the familiar and rather weary euphemisms and cliches which tend to characterise such documents. Equally it was felt that individual comments by teachers on student characteristics were doubtful in their comparability with colleagues' statements. It was therefore decided to consider four characteristics, viz. attitude/effort, initiative, behaviour in relation to teachers, and behaviour in relation to peers.

That the situation should have been of interest to a project on diagnostic assessment may be a little surprising. However, information such as this was highly compatible with the concept of Mode II diagnosis as it answered the question 'how well has the individual student learned?'. Thus, if the teacher saw as one of his aims in education the need to make a student develop his initiative and if he were able to diagnose that his student was displaying little initiative, it would be as logical to find situations in the curriculum where the student would be able to develop initiative in the same way as if he noticed that the student was unable to cut a piece of metal, he would attempt to take whatever remedial action was required.

Inevitably, however, the primary question at this stage was not 'what will you do with the information?' but 'how will you get it?'. This latter dilemma was not made easier for the researcher by existing practice in schools, for as Ingenkamp,[8] writing about research on teachers' judge-ments of personality traits, had said: '*At the moment, we have the disquieting situation in which teachers make their judgements like amateurs in the field of those objectives which are often regarded as the most important, and are subject to all those prejudices, stereotypes, distortions etc. to which all people are exposed when they have only their common sense to rely on.*'

The reporting system and the teachers' perceptions of the problem required assessment by the teachers' judgement of overt student behaviour. However, the analysis of a sample of thirty-two recording and reporting systems in Scotland for the 'Pupils in Profile' project[9] had shown that only half of the formal records included this sort of information, and so it was hardly surprising that teachers found themselves on unsure ground. Furthermore, most schools which did include the assessment of affective characteristics recorded them as a simply 'satisfactory/unsatisfactory' grade without guidelines as to meaning and, even in cases where a three-or five-point scale was used, the points were defined by simple descriptive words such as 'good', 'average' and 'poor'.

The basic problem then was to give meaning to points on the scale for the four characteristics to be assessed. The method chosen was an adaptation of Flanagan's critical incident analysis[10] which had been tried out successfully in a number of non-school training situations.[11]

A critical incident is one which can actually be seen to happen. Thus for example, 'the student shares his tools with colleagues' is a critical incident in the category 'behaviour in relation with peers'; while the statement 'good relationship with peers' is a subjective description. The teachers independently created a set of critical incidents to describe the four characteristics to be assessed. These were collated and each teacher was asked to allot each statement to what he perceived to be the correct category, and to the correct position in that category. Only those statements allotted to the correct category, and which had a high level of agreement on which point in the category scale it described, are accepted. A sequence of sifting and gap-filling phases resulted in each point on a six-point scale for each of the four student characteristics being described by at least three critical incidents. Again, there is not space here to give a full account of the process, potential and problems of the approach which are to be found in the report. Essentially, however, the teachers now had an assessment instrument which gave meaning to, say, 'effort 4', and furthermore, each teacher in the department agreed with that meaning. Of course it was not possible to create an instrument which described all behaviours associated with 'effort', but the incidents were a reliable sample of the domain of meaning attached to each point on the scale as perceived by the department. The question of how best to use the information could now be considered.

Case study three: the Mode III diagnosis of learning difficulties in geography

The work in affective student characteristics described above was one of a number of case studies where Mode III diagnostic information was provided. The test results recorded on the diagnostic record sheet designed to improve assessment in the modern languages study described above were Mode II information and the teacher was able to take reinforcement action.

In each of these studies, however, the only teaching information which could follow directly from the test result was an indication of the need or lack of it for reinforcement work, that is, for a repetition of the same sort of learning experiences, or some parallel learning experience, to the one in which the child had failed previously to come to an adequate understanding of the objective. Remedial work which focused on the reason why the student had failed to demonstrate an adequate level of understanding could only take place if the teacher worked at an individual level with the student. It was in an attempt to build in a remedial, as opposed to reinforcement, construct from the test results that Mode III diagnostic assessment was attempted.

The many questions which must be asked as to what is meant by an adequate level of understanding, and what are the theoretical underpinnings of learning, which might contribute to the creation of such tests, are of course crucial to their construction and are given attention, albeit with more questions than solutions, in the report. The case study described here, however, worked on the assumption of a very simple model which attempted to combine good teaching practice and test design.

Bloom[12] has pointed out that '*It is fortunate that schools, teachers and parents do not postpone their attempts to teach the young until an acceptable theory of learning is proclaimed and tested. Learning takes place throughout the world in the absence of an acceptable theory.*' The corollary of such a statement might be that the best place to find a good learning theory must be where successful learning is taking place; but the question which has to be asked when the search begins is how the theory is manifested. Successful teaching and, in consequence, successful learning, it is hypothesised, includes the sound inference of common errors made by students in learning any given skill, concept or element of knowledge. Teachers' experience of common errors was thus the basis of our attempt to design Mode III diagnostic tests in both modern languages and geography. A simple example from a case study in geography might serve to illustrate our approach.

A number of core concepts and skills being taught during a unit of work were selected for special attention. The teachers were asked to draw on their experience of teaching for these objectives to hypothesise the sorts of common errors which might be expected and these were built in as distractors in multiple choice items. It was hypothesised that students of the 11 to 12 year age group tended to confuse the size of the sector and the density of shading when attempting to analyse a pie graph (*Error II*). Experience suggested that this was the major error, but a minor possibility which suggested itself was that the student might refer not to the information on the graph but to some reference point in his own experience (*Error III*). Thus in question 2 where the graph suggests that half the foreign cars sold in Britain came from Russia, an alternative 'true' statement, that is, that there are more German cars sold than Russian cars, might appeal. In an attempt to verify our theory further *Error I* was designed as the reciprocal of *Error II*, that is, that given two sectors of the same size, the one with the lightest shading density would be seen as the greater. This was not hypothesised as an error, but rather it was felt that if the number of errors made in this category was as great as that made in *Error II*, we would have to treat the feedback with some scepticism.

Figure 8(iii)

The diagnostic test for pie graph interpretation and the distractor rationale

Error I	Reciprocal of Error II.
Error II	Confusion of density and sector size.
Error III	Relation to some extraneous experience rather than the 'evidence' on the pie graph.

	a	b	c	d
QUESTION I	ERROR I	ERROR II		ERROR III
2	ERROR III	ERROR II		ERROR I
3	ERROR I		ERROR III	ERROR II

Question 1
Pie graph to show the types of material used in house building

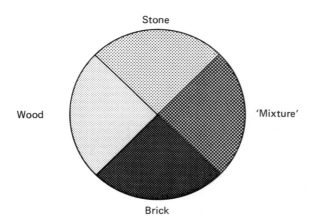

Which answer is correct?
a) There are more stone houses than brick houses.
b) There are more brick houses than stone houses.
c) There is the same number of brick and stone houses.
d) There are more 'mixture' houses than wood houses.

Question 2
Pie graph to show where foreign cars sold in Britain come from

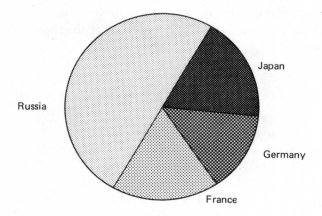

Which answer is correct?
a) There are more German cars than Russian cars.
b) There are more Japanese cars than French cars.
c) There is the same number of Japanese cars as French cars.
d) There are more French cars than Japanese cars.

Question 3
Pie graph to show the kind of people in a town

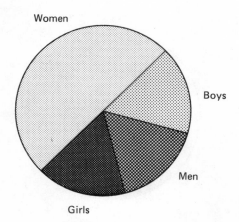

Which answer is correct?
a) There are more boys than girls in the town.
b) There is the same number of boys and girls in the town.
c) There is the same number of men and women in the town.
d) There are more girls than boys in the town.

As the analysis of responses shown on Figure 8(iv) suggests, our hypothesis that *Error II* (confusion of sector size and shading density) was a common misconception among the students seems sound. More than 6 per cent of the students chose the *Error II* option consistently, while another 6 per cent made the error twice out of three. It is worth noting that the probability of choosing the *Error II* distractor on each occasion by chance was 0.016 and even the probability of two consistent errors out of three was 0.06. Equally, the unpopularity of *Error I* in comparison to *Error II*, especially in the three items choice column, would seem to be evidence in support of the hypothesised error. *Error III*, however, did not appear to be common amongst the students and those few students who did appear to make the error would probably require individual investigation by the teachers before remedial action was taken.

What information can the teacher take from such a test? To begin with, he must be aware that we do not yet have adequate statistical methods of analysing items for content validity. However, where students consistently choose responses in parallel items when these responses have been constructed from teachers' experience of error and where the incidence of these responses is significantly removed from the statistical probability of chance, it would seem reasonable to assume that we may have good items. The issue is complex and the safest assumption that we can make is that by sampling the students' understanding of pie graphs we have indications that will tell us how best to proceed. For two hundred and twenty of the pupils in our sample, our strategy should be to move on; for thirty-nine others, a remedial exercise is required which will make them aware that the size of the sector indicates relative importance; while for the remaining fifty-eight the teacher may provide reinforcement work. Furthermore, with a little systematic investigation, he may discover the reasons for their misunderstanding and so build further distractors into his diagnostic test next time round.

Conclusion

These three case studies in diagnostic assessment highlight my earlier assertion that formative assessment should be clearly differentiated from the criticisms which are often made of assessment in general. The potential result of looking more closely at how we follow our students'

CLASS	3r	2r	3I	2I	3II	2II	3III	2III	RANDOM	3 N.A.	2 N.A.
1A	11	10	0	0	4	1	0	0	2	0	0
1B	8	13	0	1	2	1	0	0	2	0	0
1C	6	6	0	2	0	2	0	0	4	0	1
1D	11	11	0	1	0	1	0	0	3	0	0
1E	12	11	0	0	2	2	0	0	0	0	0
1G	7	13	0	1	1	1	0	0	4	0	0
1H	5	6	0	0	3	4	0	1	3	0	0
1L	7	10	0	2	2	3	0	0	3	0	0
1M	9	11	0	0	2	0	0	1	2	0	0
1N	8	9	0	0	3	2	0	1	1	0	0
1R	9	10	0	3	0	0	0	0	4	0	0
1V	7	10	0	1	1	2	0	2	4	0	0
TOTAL	100	121	0	11	20	19	0	5	32	0	1

RESPONSE TO QUESTIONS

Figure 8(iv)   An analysis of the responses to the three questions on pie graphs

progress is exponential. By removing the hurdle construct from assessment we create the situation where both student and teacher will begin to see it as a positive contribution to learning. We will be in a position to extend the concept of remedial education to the whole population.

How then does diagnostic assessment relate to summative assessment? In truth there is a dilemma. On the one hand, the sort of information offered by diagnostic assessment is potentially of great value to any reporting system. On the other, the danger of associating diagnostic assessment with reporting is that it will be construed as a hurdle with all that this implies.

Nevertheless, society demands that schools sort students and this is unlikely to change. But diagnostic assessment and student statements have at least one thing in common, which is their very essence – they are both primarily focused on the strengths and weaknesses of the individual. If the positive learning oriented feedback, which is fundamental to diagnostic assessment, can be the commonsense meaning of assessment in the future and if society's hurdle can be relegated to an important but subsidiary by-product of learning, then the two will ably complement each other. However, if any form of terminal assessment continues to dominate education to the detriment of learning, little progress will be made.

References

1 Ingenkamp, K. *Educational Assessment* NFER, Slough, 1977
2 Petch, J. A. *GGE & Degree, Part I.* Occasional Publications 10, JMB, 1961
3 Barnett, V. D. & Lewis, T. 'A study of the relationship between GCE & degree results', *J. of the Royal Statistical Soc.*, Series A (General), 1963, 126, 2, 187–226
4 Entwistle, N., Nisbet, J., Entwistle, P. & Cowell, M. 'The academic performance of students', *Br. Journal Ed. Psychol.*, 1971, 41, 3, 258–78
5 Powell, J. L. *Selection for University in Scotland*, The Scottish Council for Research in Education, Edinburgh, 1975
6 Scottish Council for Research in Education. Diagnostic Assessment Project: forthcoming reports (1979)
7 Ingenkamp, K. op. cit.
8 Ingenkamp, K. op. cit.
9 *Pupils in Profile* (see Broadfoot's paper, note 10), 1977
10 Flanagan, J. C. 'A new approach to evaluating personnel', in *Personnel* 1949, 26, 35–42
11 e.g. Smith, P. C. & Kendall, L. M. 'Retranslation of Expectations', *J. App. Psychol.*, 1963, 47, 149–155
12 Bloom, B. *Human Characteristics & School Learning* McGraw Hill, 1976

9 Bringing education back into schools

JOHN RAVEN

This chapter is in four parts. The first asserts, on the basis of research evidence, that post-primary education is no longer concerned with growth and development. The second attributes this, not to the failings of teachers, but to the effects of the education system, particularly in assessing and certifying. The third identifies the problems that must be overcome if a better system is to be evolved. The fourth describes indications of the way in which this might be done.

Part One

When teachers, students, parents and employers have been asked to say what the main goals of education are, most have agreed that they are to develop our most human capacities: the ability to learn without instruction, the ability to make one's own observations, the ability to live and work with others, and the ability to care for one's community (Johnson and Bachman, 1976; Morton-Williams *et al.*, 1968; Morton-Williams, Raven and Ritchie, 1970; Raven *et al.*, 1975, 1976, 1977). Nevertheless, teachers and students, both in Britain and in the United States, report that these goals receive almost no attention in secondary education. As Bronfenbrenner (1974) has put it, we have lost the ability to make human beings human.

As research by the author and his colleagues has shown, teachers at the present time feel obliged to goad their students in an autocratic manner to work toward examination goals in which they do not themselves believe, and which they think confer few benefits on them. They do this because, unless students pass academic, knowledge-based examinations, their future life chances will be placed in jeopardy. As a result, schools have become not developing environments but stultifying environments. Thirty per cent of secondary school boys in Scotland get the belt every fortnight (Pollock, 1977). How can it possibly be maintained that this environment is designed to foster the human qualities of which we have spoken? Only 18 per cent of American secondary school students say that they are able to develop and utilise their talents at school, compared with 80 per cent of those employed in factory work (Johnson and

Bachman, 1976). More than half of the students interviewed in Great Britain and Ireland by the author and his colleagues felt that more than half of their subjects were both boring and useless. More than a quarter wanted more to be done to achieve 90 per cent of the objectives we asked them about (Raven, 1977). Students have reacted against their demeaning, antigrowth environments by truancy, vandalism and refusal to 'work'. To attempt to stamp out this protest reaction might involve trying to stamp out the very potential for development of the human race.

Part Two

The research studies we have summarised in the last paragraph show that teachers' hearts are in the right place. Their over-riding concern is to help their students to develop their most human qualities. But, as the same research shows, they are prevented from doing so by the pernicious effects of an examination system, which, counter to the better judgement of most teachers, students and parents, overwhelmingly determines what goes on in schools. Some authors (for example Shipman, 1971) have maintained that the school system is a microcosm of society, and that the school system of a capitalist society necessarily has to prepare students for subservient roles in boring and routine jobs; but what is maintained here is something very different. My argument is that the terrifying situation just reported has come about for the best of motives. Students were trapped into the school system, not because it was felt that prolonged imprisonment in a stultifying environment would prepare them for life as a robot in a machine-minded society, but because we were anxious that they should become self-respecting individuals who would *not* be trapped into demeaning occupations. Academic credentials were used in the process of job allocation, not because selection of those who did well in them was thought to be a guarantee of willingness to work at soul-destroying tasks, but because we were anxious to select the most able members of our soceity for the most important jobs by means of the most objective criteria, which were least likely to reflect biases from the student's home background and the school he attended. Had we had available to us objective measures of qualities like resourcefulness, initiative, leadership abilities, and ability to learn from experience there is little doubt that these would have been included in the selection process.

Surveys carried out among employers and students (Raven and Dolphin, 1978; Raven, unpublished) show that they would be happy for assessments of these and other qualities to be included on school certificates.

Teachers, however (Raven *et al.*, 1975) are much less happy about this suggestion, partly because they are ambivalent about the value issues involved, but mainly because they have not fully considered the sociological functions performed by the educational system and asked themselves how these functions can be brought to push them in the direction in which they want to go. They wish to escape those sociological functions altogether.

They may be right. If legislation were enacted to prohibit employers from selecting employees at any level, including university graduates, unless there was explicit evidence demonstrating the validity of the credentials they used in predicting future occupational performance, that would indeed markedly reduce the constraints on teachers' behaviour.

Nevertheless, despite the apparently attractive nature of this solution, the fact remains that, if our society is to recognise, foster and utilise the talents available to it, it will be necessary for those concerned with recognising and fostering to have available to them reliable and valid means of assessing the qualities which were mentioned in the first paragraph. The remainder of this chapter will, therefore, be devoted to outlining some of the problems to be faced if better means of assessing progress toward the main goals of education are to be developed, and some directions which may be followed in search of a solution.

Part Three

The model of the intellect

There are a large number of problems to be overcome if an appropriate system of assessment is to be developed. These include, first, the need to change the model of the intellect which has informed discussion in education for the last quarter of a century. Most teachers assume that if a student is good at one thing he will be good at another (Raven *et al.*, 1976). And psychologists have generally supported them in this thinking. Indeed, there *is* a 'general factor' in academic abilities – but some of the correlations are only of the order of 0.3, leaving some 91 per cent of the variance in students' scores on one variable unpredictable from their scores on the other. But these correlations drop still further when one considers abilities like judgement, forecasting ability and leadership. These abilities, and still others, including the ability to articulate group goals and unleash the abilities of others in pursuing them, creativity, ability to put others at their ease, and willingness to act with the long term interest of society in mind, appear to be very little related to general intelligence and academic ability. It is therefore necessary for us to start to work with a multiple-ability concept of talent. Furthermore, there are so many of these talents that it is impossible for any one individual to develop more than a fraction of them to the fullest extent possible. Yet society needs some individuals possessed of each of these talents. We need some fine analytic thinkers, some social activists, some whose forte it is to get other people to pull together, and so on.

If the argument of the last paragraph is accepted, it is inappropriate to put all students through courses geared to similar objectives or to measure them all against the same, or similar, criteria. They all have to develop their own idiosyncratic talents and be measured against idiosyncratic criteria. This fact is, of course, recognised in some forms of project-based education in which an effort is made to encourage some students to develop the ability to encourage co-operation, others to become knowledge resources, others to become inventors, and so on. All students master different bodies of academic knowledge related to their own interests.

The implications of our argument for employers is that their task becomes that of deciding which talents they need and thereafter asking themselves how they can get employees into positions in which they can utilise and develop their talents. Their task is *not* to select the 'most able' people.

This potential solution to the problem is obviously inimical to our current examination system, in which all students are graded in terms of a very small number of closely related criteria so that there can be a 'fair' competition for high status jobs and all that goes with them. Our argument points in what some would take to be a backward-looking direction: to the need for teachers to return to an assessment system in which they specify each student's particular strengths.

Competencies involve values
A second major barrier to be overcome if we are to develop a more appropriate certification system has to do with the fact that qualities like initiative, leadership, ability to work with others and responsibility will only be displayed by individuals, and therefore practised and developed, if the individuals are working towards goals they value. For example, a great deal of time and energy is required to take effective initiatives. One has to mull over the fleeting feelings of unease which indicate that one has a problem which was not previously recognised as such, one has to mull over the strategies to be used to persuade others to help one tackle the problem, one has to try out solutions and monitor their effectiveness in order to learn more about what one is dealing with, and one has to summon up the energy required to initiate corrective action. One cannot expect anyone to display such high levels of energy and commitment in relation to goals they do not care about. And if they do not practise such behaviour they will not become more competent at it.

Similarly, such qualities can only be assessed in relation to goals which the individual values. It does not make sense to say that someone is unable to communicate, to help other people, to take initiative, to anticipate future events, or learn without instruction, if he does not value the goal towards which we expect him to work, and in the course of trying to achieve which he is expected by us to display these qualities. He may be perfectly well able to display these qualities in relation to some other goals which he does value. Educationists have too often been guilty of saying that an individual lacks the ability to perform some task, when, in reality, they are really saying that he is unwilling to exercise that ability in circumstances which he does not himself consider to be fruitful.

It follows from what has been said that if we are to assess these qualities we must, as Stansbury shows, first assess the styles of behaviour the person values and the sort of person he wants to be. And here is a dilemma. For, in our society, we are highly ambivalent about values: as we have seen, virtually everyone is agreed that the main objective of the educational system is to influence values. But the notion of doing so explicitly and systematically makes us all feel very uneasy.

The point to be made here is that if, as we do, we wish to foster the most important and human attributes of our children and adult members of our society, we must face this problem. Dangerous and open to abuse though it is, the only way to place educational policy, indeed all social policy, on a more rational footing is to come to terms with it.

The need is to assess competencies, not knowledge of content
A third problem is that new measurement theory is required to assess such qualities. The techniques of educational assessment which have so far been 'perfected' (though, heaven help us, many of these are of doubtful enough validity – see Ingenkamp, 1977) mainly enable us to assess knowledge of content. Yet most of the qualities we have mentioned in this chapter are best thought of as broadly based styles of behaviour. Knowledge of subject matter enters into them hardly at all. And they are somehow more than skills or arts, for they pervade every aspect of our day-to-day living. Every day one follows, leads, invents, observes, plans and thinks. They differ from skills in another way too. They are proactive, self-motivated, rather than re-active. It does not make sense to say that someone has shown initiative if he has been told what to do and how to do it. More than that, successful initiatives involve striving over a long period, planning, anticipating obstacles, getting help from others, continuously monitoring what is going on for what it tells one about the problem one is dealing with, and taking corrective action where necessary. The ability to do these things involves great sensitivity to flickering feelings of unease on the fringe of consciousness which contain a

germ of a new pertinent observation, a new insight, idea, or an indication of how to improve one's behaviour.

The conclusion to which this discussion leads us is this: these complex qualities have very little in common with the knowledge of content which is mainly assessed in school examinations. But neither are these qualities adequately described as 'skills'. They involve complex, integrated, cognitive, affective and behavioural styles.

The best word I can find to refer to them is 'competency'. The key shift which is required in education – and in educational assessment – is, therefore, from a focus on *content* to a focus on *competencies*.

Educated abilities should be 'normally' distributed

A fourth problem has to deal with the fact that, while abilities in their un-educated state may possibly be expected to be 'normally' distributed, educated abilities should be distributed according to the chart below

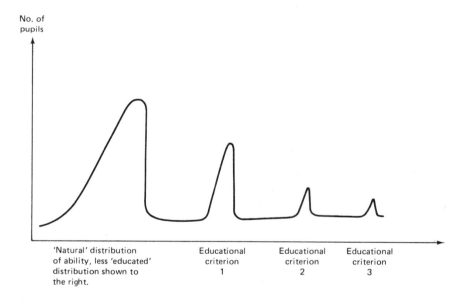

Level of ability in specified area.

where groups of students have been brought to the levels of mastery indicated by the peaks in the tail of the distribution. A 'normal' distribution of 'educated' abilities represents an indictment of the school system. Either the teachers concerned do not really believe that all their students need to master what they are teaching, or they have done a wholly inadequate job of teaching it. Either way, a 'normal' distribution is an inducement to reform teaching practice, not an opportunity to distinguish between pupils in terms of 'ability'.

Part Four

There are a number of promising ways in which assessments of students' ability and willingness to engage in complex behaviours, related to goals which they themselves value, might be improved. Nevertheless, the tools available to us do not enable us to handle the problem to which attention was drawn at the start of this chapter. Because the relevant information can so easily be falsified, the available assessment techniques do not enable us to select some individuals for privileged positions in society and to relegate others to the scrap heap. They do enable us, if society were to commit itself to developing, using and rewarding all the talents available to it, to find ways of enabling individuals to develop and use their talents for the benefit of society as a whole. They do, in short, enable us to work towards an adequate system of guidance, placement and development of individuals and organisations, whether these are schools, firms or society. The techniques are of three main kinds, based on structured student self-ratings, projective techniques and teacher ratings. These techniques are described in more detail in Raven (1977); all that it is possible to do here is to indicate briefly the nature of what is possible and, I hope, to whet the reader's appetite. Despite this latter desire, however, the summaries which follow are necessarily technical.

Structured student self-ratings: value expectancy measures

Students may be asked systematically to report what would happen if they were to engage in the high level behaviours of which we have spoken – taking responsibility, persuading others, trying to make their views known to others, pursuing a store of unrivalled technical expertise in a particular area – in relation to a goal they value.

Students are first asked what the personal consequences would be if, for example, they tried to persuade their fellow students to behave in a more responsible manner. They may, for example (and often do) think that trying to do this would make them uncomfortable and unhappy, leave them less time for other activities they value, and demand abilities which they do not possess. In the absence of these abilities any attempt on their part to persuade other people to behave in this way would demand a great deal of effort, lead them to think that others would feel that they were getting above themselves and end up by being an ignominious failure. They would look, in their own eyes, and in the eyes of others, very foolish indeed.

After asking them what they think the general consequences would be, they are asked whether the sort of person they would like to be would do this – and what sort of person would do it. They may, for example, feel that the sort of person who would try to persuade his fellow students to behave more responsibly would be a rather pious, priggish killjoy, and that to be successful they would have to be devious and manipulative. They may not wish to be any of these things.

Finally, they are asked how others would react: would their friends support or reject them, would their teachers condemn them because they would have exposed teachers' behaviour as self-interested, rather than concerned with the good of their students; will they, like Socrates, be deprived of a livelihood for having been concerned about the long-term social consequences of their actions?

To take another example: striving to improve one's school to make it a more educational environment may be thought to involve endless frustration, loss of examination credentials, inability to persuade fellow students and staff to cooperate, and ostracism by teachers and fellow students alike. Such a set of perceptions and expectations hardly incline one to believe that the individual concerned would engage in the behaviour.

If one cumulated these results one would have a clear assessment of the individual's disinclination to engage in these activities.

But one would have a great deal more than that, for one would have a lot of material which would be of value in helping one to devise an individualised, competency based programme of education designed to help the individual, if he so wished, to develop a greater tendency and ability to behave in this way. He could, for example, be brought to pay more attention to the probable long-term social consequences of his not taking such responsibility. He might be brought into contact with other young people who had behaved in a responsible way and not been punished or forced to behave in ways which were contrary to their self-image. By becoming familiar with them he might learn how to persuade other people more effectively without becoming obnoxious. He could be helped to practise the skills required to obtain the cooperation of others.

Not only would the information be of value in making it possible to design an *individual* programme of development for this particular pupil, it would, if collected from a wider sample of students, be of great value in enabling a school, or a school system, to assess the adequacy of its overall programme of general education and thereafter greatly improve it.

To summarise this discussion in more abstract terms, the procedure we have described enables one to collect information which: reveals an individual's values, concerns and interests (so that a relevant individualised programme of development and placement can be evolved for him); yields an index of the strength of the individual's tendency to engage in the high level competencies which are being assessed; draws attention to the individual's idiosyncratic educational needs; and draws attention to systems defects which may require the attention of an organisational psychologist or sociologist rather than an educator. The potential of the model for collecting the information required as a basis for educational programmes, for assessing the impact of educational programmes, in fostering changed expectations and patterns of competence, and for specifying organisational changes which are required if the institution of society is to tap the goodwill, knowhow and initiative which is available to it is, therefore, considerable. Further details of the exact procedure to be followed will be found in Raven (1977) and Raven and Dolphin (1978).

Projective techniques

The term 'projective test' is used to cover a wide range of tests which vary greatly in their theoretical basis and scoring procedure. A feature shared by most is that they sample the testees' reactions to a given stimulus. The stimulus may be a picture, an unfinished sentence, or something similar. Of particular value from the point of view of making rough assessments of whether groups of individuals are likely to engage spontaneously in a number of the types of competent behaviour, which were identified earlier in relation to goals they value, are tests built around the scoring system developed by McClelland (1958). These are particularly valuable for assessing the impact of educational programmes and for helping teachers to clarify the nature of the competencies they wish to foster and the means to be used to foster them.

McClelland's procedure is to show his informants a short series of, say, six pictures. The pictures may depict students of roughly the same age as the pupils being tested in a variety of situations which are of interest to the educator. After looking briefly at each picture the students are asked to make up a story about what the characters in the picture are thinking, feeling and doing; what led up to the situation, what is happening, and what the outcome will be. The pictures that are used have to be carefully selected to provide cues to the sort of thoughts, feelings and actions in which the educator is interested. The stories are then carefully examined to see whether there is any evidence that the writer thinks that his characters spend time making plans, anticipating obstacles, getting the help of others, striving to reach their goals for long periods, turning their emotions into what they are doing and enjoying their work. It is assumed that if the writer of the story thinks that his characters do these things, he will tend to do them himself. Let us take an example. Supposing one takes 'consideration for others' as an example, the first question that comes to mind is 'what specific pictures should be used?' This question is very important educationally since it forces the teachers or researchers concerned to think about the sorts of situation in which the pattern of thoughts, feelings and behaviours which they describe as 'considerateness' may or may not be elicited. There are many situations in which the tendency to engage in 'considerate behaviour' would be highly inappropriate. On the other hand there are situations in which everyone would be expected to display this characteristic. Although pictures falling at these extremes are of little use in assessment, they tell one a great deal about the environmental characteristics which lead people to engage in the cognitive, affective and behavioural pattern with which one is concerned. This information provides a stimulus to thinking about situations in which the patterns of thought, feeling and behaviour in which one is interested can be elicited, and these, in turn, can be used as a starting point for experience-based learning programmes designed to generate these behaviour patterns and help those involved analyse the components of their behaviour.

Once suitable photographs have been obtained, suitable in the sense of depicting situations in which one would like the characteristic (considerateness) to be displayed, but in which it may not be displayed, one has to devise a scoring system.

Essentially, such a scoring system, designed to measure the spontaneous tendency to engage in these ways of behaving, should encourage those who are using it look for the following characteristics.

It should encourage scorers to look for four things: first, explicit statements of concern with the characteristic: statements that the characters in the stories want to display it, positive statements that the characters did not display it when they should have done, and so on; second, references to relevant behaviour – the characters in the stories were engaging in this behaviour, they had done it before, they were giving or receiving help in performing relevant tasks; third, cognitive elements – the characters may have made contingency plans to deal with the situation, they may anticipate obstacles to the effective execution of the course of action they wish to undertake, they may not know how to go about it and so on; fourth, expressions which reveal a tendency on the part of the subject to turn his emotions into the behavioural pattern – does he, for example, see the characters in his stories feeling good or bad about their behaviour, anticipating the outcomes of their activity (or inactivity) with feeling?

Having once devised such a scoring system it will be necessary for the investigators to check the statistical reliability of their scoring procedure. This will probably serve to give them a salutary shock and cause them to go over their scoring system – the characteristics they are looking for in the stories (and seeking to foster in their students) – in more detail. If it turns out to be impossible to obtain reliable measures it follows that the words we are using either lack all meaning or describe behaviours which are characteristic of people in certain situations rather than characteristic of certain people in many situations. If the latter turns out to be the case, and if our group have gone about their task seriously, their efforts will not have been in vain, since they will have learned a great deal about the sorts of situations which encourage and release the sorts of behaviour in which they are interested. If the behaviours in which they are interested are indeed important in educational and organisational situations the group will therefore have learned something of the greatest importance. All that will have happened is that the exercise will have contributed to the group's understanding of the situational determinants of behaviour instead of to their understanding of personal characteristics. As was previously indicated the two are conceptually separable but, in spite of what many research studies would lead one to believe, inextricably interconnected in practice. But note the catch: to test one's hypothesis that such qualities are situationally specific one needs measures of whether individuals display these qualities more in some situations than in others.

Lest the reader be deterred from experimenting with these measures by what he has heard of their 'unreliability', attention may be drawn to a number of points. First, only one, very specific, form of projective methodology is being advocated here. Second, just as the value-expectancy 'measures' described above were factorially complex, so too are these measures. Third, there are two major problems to overcome even if one approaches the question of validity from the point of view of conventional psychometric thinking. First, human beings tend not to go on thinking about a problem once they have solved it. Thus, if an individual grapples with one of his problems in his first story, he is unlikely to return to it in his second story, or on a subsequent occasion. Nor is he likely to be preoccupied with a host of problems at any one time. A low split-half or re-test reliability for the measure therefore tells one surprisingly little. Second, as we have already seen, different people may choose to display their competence in very different ways and in very different circumstances. Very broad criteria, or case histories, are therefore needed if any attempt is to be made to validate such measures.

Teacher ratings

Procedures are available which enable us to develop much more systematic teacher-rating procedures which take into account the sort of problems outlined earlier. Nevertheless, if they are to be useful, it is essential simultaneously to change the teaching situations created in schools in such a way that students can practise, develop and display the sorts of qualities we have mentioned. Paradoxically, because of the role which certification systems play in shaping the curriculum, such situations can only be created when better assessment procedures have been developed.

The normal defects of teacher ratings are, first, that teachers rarely give their students much opportunity to show whether they are able to engage in the high level behaviours discussed in this chapter and, second, that they disagree amongst themselves about what behaviour should count as evidence of a particular quality. As has been indicated, the first of these problems can be solved only by changing the educational processes which go on in the classroom (but working on the development of better *measures* of these qualities leads many more people to appreciate the need to change educational practice). The second problem can, with difficulty, be solved by having groups of teachers systematically evaluate their use of such terms and agree on the behaviour which will be taken to indicate the presence or absence of a particular quality. In this case the relevant procedures were originally developed by Smith and Kendall (1963) and have again been summarised, in more detail than is given here, in Raven (1977).

In the construction of such rating scales a group of teachers first tries to make the objectives they are seeking to pursue more explicit. The group then makes a conceptual analysis of these objectives in order to reduce the number. Some of the more crucial are then selected for further study. For each of these each member of the group next writes 'critical incidents' describing behaviours they have seen real people display in the past and which they themselves think illustrate a particularly high or a particularly low level of the characteristic. Instances of intermediate levels of the characteristic are also obtained. In all cases the actual behaviour of the individual must be recorded, together with a description of what led the individual to engage in it, and what happened afterwards. The situational elements of the behaviour – which are so useful in structuring learning situations in which the behaviour will be engaged in and practised – are again thereby emphasised.

The group then divides into two. Each sub-group looks at the incidents they have written and discusses whether or not they relate to the dimensions to which they are supposed to relate. In the process two things are discovered. First, it is impossible to produce examples of behaviour which illustrate some of the dimensions, with the implication that either nothing is being done by the schools concerned to encourage the students to engage in, practise and develop the patterns of thinking, feeling and behaving described by the term, or that the term itself has no real meaning. If we cannot tell whether a characteristic is present or absent how can it be a useful means of describing individual differences in behaviour? Second, some of the incidents do not fit into the conceptual framework which has been evolved.

Discussion of these problems leads to refinement of the conceptual framework. Some dimensions are abandoned. Others are replaced. Others are clarified. And others are added.

Eventually a set of dimensions is agreed upon by each group. Each dimension is indexed by a set of incidents which are agreed to be unambiguously related to the dimension. The incidents are now ranked in order from say $+5$ through 0 to -5, according to whether the individual who engaged in the behaviour is thought to display a high level of the characteristic or its opposite. Again, items about which there is disagreement are abandoned. Now some scale points turn out to be represented by many items whilst others are blank. For the latter an attempt is made to think of real incidents to fill the gaps. Eventually each group has an agreed set of dimensions each indexed by an orderly set of incidents.

Now comes a crucial stage in the procedure. The groups remove all markings indicating either the dimension or scale point from the items and hand the items to the other group. The task of each member of the other group is now to assign each item to the dimensional framework and to assess its appropriate scale point. Any item about which there is disagreement between the two groups concerning either the characteristic displayed or the degree of the characteristic has to be abandoned. The average of the ratings finally gives the scale position of the behaviour depicted in the critical incident. Ideally each dimension is now operationally defined in terms of real behaviour ranging from $+5$ to -5. The final stage, intended to enable raters to make use of their general knowledge of their ratee's behaviour tendencies, and thus enable them to make reasonable assessments of behaviour tendencies which they may not actually have observed in practice, is to prefix each item with 'would be expected to . . .'. The final instrument, which can be used to rate anybody, consists of rating scales for a number of dimensions, the scale points on each scale being quite specific in behavioural terms.

To obtain the maximum benefit from such an exercise the participants should subsequently focus on what led them to abandon certain items and concepts. Discussion of this material will lead them to become much clearer about the situational pressures which lead people to behave in one way on one occasion and in another way on another occasion. As was particularly clear when we discussed value-expectancy theory, the willingness to engage in many socially important behaviours may derive more from the situation in which the individual is placed than from his previous experience or personal characteristics. Knowledge of the variables which release these behaviours may be of the utmost importance both socially and educationally.

Conclusion

As will already have become apparent, the merits of the three assessment systems outlined above are not confined to assessment. Teachers who strive to develop such measures inevitably develop a much better understanding of the nature of the qualities they wish to foster and thereby gain new insights into ways in which they are to be fostered. If assessments of such qualities were incorporated into the school certification system, additional benefits would accrue because of the need to devise a system of external moderation which would require one teacher to stand over his colleagues' assessments of qualities which he himself may not be concerned to foster. The qualities which it is most important to assess are often described as process goals, and these process goals, such as fostering initiative, leadership, and the ability to formulate the nature of a problem, rarely leave an adequate trace in the end product of the activity. By definition, such qualities can only be observed by observing the educational process itself. If teachers are to be brought to stand over their fellow teachers' assessments of students' progress toward such goals they will have to be heavily involved in discussion of these goals, the methods to be used to attain them, and the behaviours that are to count as evidence of the process being engaged in. The structures required to promote such development of understanding would be extremely beneficial to the process of education itself. And, as we have seen, *unless* we develop means of giving teachers and students credit for working towards such process goals, most of them will continue to neglect the most important objectives of education. As we have said, this is not malicious behaviour on their part. It is a product of placing them in a system which deflects them from their goals. Enabling them to achieve the goals which they themselves hold most dear involves modifying the credentialling system in such a way that it gives both the teachers and students concerned credit for having worked toward these goals. In this chapter we have outlined the beginnings of a set of measurement procedures, and a certification *system*, which would enable this to be done.

References

Bronfenbrenner, U., *The Origins of Alienation*, Scientific American 231, pp. 53–61, 1974

Ingenkamp, K., *Educational Assessment*, NFER, 1977

Johnson, L. D. & Bachman, J. G., *Educational Institutions and Adolescent Development* in Adams, James (ed.) *Understanding Adolescence*, Allyn & Baker, Boston, 1976

McClelland, D. C. (with Atkinson, J.), *Motives in Fantasy, Action and Society*, 1958

Morton-Williams, R. *et al.*, *Young School Leavers*, HMSO, 1968

Morton-Williams, R. *et al.*, *Sixth Form Teachers and Pupils*, for Schools Council by Books for Schools Ltd, 1970

Pollock, G. J. *et al.*, *Report to EIS on Pupils' Attitudes to School Rules and Punishments*, Scottish Council for Research in Education, 1977

Raven, J. *et al.*, *Pupils' Perceptions of Educational Objectives and their Reactions to School and School Subjects*, Irish Association for Curriculum Development, Dublin, 1975

Raven, J., *Teachers' Perceptions of Educational Objectives and Examinations*, Irish Association for Curriculum Development, Dublin, 1975

Raven, J., *Pupil Motivation and Values*, Irish Association for Curriculum Development, Dublin, 1976

Raven, J., *Education, Values and Society*, H. K. Lewis, London, The Psychological Corporation, New York, 1977

Raven, J. and Dolphin, T., *The Consequences of Behaving*, Competency Motivation Project, Edinburgh, 1978

Shipman, M. D., *Education and Modernisation*, Allen & Unwin, 1971

Smith, P. C. & Kendall, L. M., *Retranslation of Expectations*, Journal of Applied Psychology 47, pp. 149–155, 1963

Note: the views expressed in this chapter are those of the author and do not necessarily reflect those of the Scottish Council for Research in Education.

10   Primary school records:
St Anne's First School

ELSA DAVIES

Although this book is mostly concerned with the secondary stage of education the following contribution concerns the process of recording pupil progress at the other end of the educational spectrum. After a brief history, a detailed account is given of the current practice at a first school where record-keeping is part of a strategy of individual development. Emphasis is placed upon the advantages of pupil involvement and parent participation. The stages in the development of this 'open' system serve to show how decisions taken about school records have contributed to pupil, parent and teacher preparation for the future.

The background

Looking back to 1965 when I began my teaching career in a small primary school in South Wales, I cannot remember any discussion taking place about individual notes on pupils. It is possible that official local authority record cards were kept but, as a class teacher, I was never aware of their presence in the school. A system of informal school records did not exist: perhaps such informal notes were thought to be unnecessary for at the age of eleven years the pupils entered a selective external examination which appeared to give an assessment of the progress which each individual had made. It was from sheer necessity and, sadly, without any support from the head teacher, that I devised a simple system of personal, *aide-memoire* style notes about my infant-aged pupils.

Following on this experience, it was my good fortune to enjoy a brief period of teaching at a seconday school, where I learnt from the professional side about the workings of the school report system. Although such a system has many disadvantages, not the least of which is the inadequacy of brief phrases about a pupil, it does provide some sort of information for parents. Whether the considerable effort expended upon termly reports is directed to a fruitful end for all concerned is a matter of debate and merits the consideration of all thinking teachers.

In 1970 I began work as a deputy head teacher of a moderately sized infants school in one of the Greater London boroughs. Here, for the first time in my career, I saw a system of formal and informal school records on pupils. The informal records consisted of a cumulative series of comments by the child's teachers, a number record and a dated reading book achievement record. Despite the fact that all these records were stored in separate places, the important point was that records were kept. In addition, end-of-year notes were also prepared with details of the child's present level of achievement ready for the pupil's new teacher at the start of each academic year. As far as the formal record was concerned the class teachers of the oldest transferring pupils were responsible, following consultation with the head teacher, for compiling the appropriate infant school record paragraph on the official card.

All the previous information serves to illustrate the point that when I took up my present position as head teacher of a Group Five First School in the County of Surrey in 1974, my knowledge of the process of recording pupil progress was, to put it mildly, rather limited. Yet there I was, not only responsible for ensuring the pupils' academic advancement but also for monitoring that progress and providing some record of it. It would have helped me to have known more of Surrey's history, tradition and 'ways of working', but a specific problem presented itself. My new school was sited in what was originally the old County of Middlesex and although the amalgamation of the area into Surrey had taken place in 1965, the attitudinal ethos of Middlesex still remained strong. I understood from the start that our area was somewhat 'special' and certainly 'different' from the rest of Surrey. Perhaps because of this, little was done to fill in the past history of Surrey, as opposed to Middlesex, in general matters and specifically in the area of pupil documentation. Yet Surrey has quite a distinguished history in a number of fields including that of pupil records. This, I have discovered, is largely due to the able and enthusiastic leadership of the local authority inspectorate over the years. As regards the formation and development of pupil records they have, during the past thirty years, encouraged a high degree of teacher involvement. The production of the Pupils Record Card in 1947 led to in-service courses for teachers in the theoretical background to recording and training in skills necessary for the effective use of the Card. The gatherings of heads and teachers on these occasions grew into the Surrey Educational Research Association which was set up in 1947 and incorporated into the Surrey Schools Council in 1966. Up to the present day, professional discussion on pupil record keeping remains in the forefront, and the tradition of grass roots teacher involvement continues.

In the school, the position regarding official County pupil records left much to be desired. After a few weeks as head, I discovered that there were no new Surrey Pupils Record Cards available and that, to offset this deficiency, a group of eight local head teachers, including my predecessor, had cooperated to design and fund the printing of a record card for use in our schools. Although it bore the title Surrey County Council Confidential Record, it did not receive official County blessing. Still in use, this card is far from perfect; it suffers from most of the faults of similar, old-style cards, yet only in September 1978 is it beginning to be phased out by the introduction of the latest official Surrey Education Committee Pupils Record.

This new Pupils Record incorporates what were once called the teacher's informal notes on a pupil. At the school there were some of these pupil records left by the previous head, but I found nothing older than three years. My predecessor had begun the task by initiating a number record sheet, a reading book/phonic list and general development notes for each pupil. These three items were all kept in separate places and the latter notes were written on postcards. One of my first major tasks, therefore, was to achieve a form of pupil profile which would allow all the information on each pupil to be drawn together. After quite considerable staff discussion and liaison with our Middle School, we produced a format of a profile which included reading, writing and phonic records, a number progress sheet, a behaviour profile and pages for the teacher's comments on social and emotional development. These sheets were stapled together with a front cover of general factual information and a back page indicating the names of teachers who had taught the pupil. We added to this profile any psychologist's or school doctor's reports or relevant parent letters, such as requests that their child should be excused from drinking milk or had special dietary needs. The profiles were kept separate from the formal record cards and were stored in alphabetical index files in a central place. Each autumn and at the end of the school year, these records were updated and every July we forwarded the profiles of the transferring pupils to the Middle School, along with their formal record cards.

Although these profiles coordinated pupil information in a better way than the previous head teacher's system, they left much room for improvement. Their first major disadvantage was that they were not put to good use by the staff. The teachers did not often refer to the profiles to help or guide them in their approach to individual pupils. Yet it was the second major disadvantage of these profiles which led to our re-thinking and redesigning their format. Over recent years there had been a tremendous growth in the amount and quality of parent involvement at the school and it did not seem appropriate in a partnership of openness in cooperation to maintain the secrecy of pupil documents. These old-style profiles were not available to parents and, as a staff, we felt that parents had a right of access to them. Rather than merely declare open access to the current profile, we felt it to be a suitable opportunity to reassess the merits of the whole document and its role as a meaningful evaluation of the pupil.

Present experience

Our profiles were changed more in the physical sense than in the actual content. The updated version is enclosed in a sugar paper folder which is coloured according to the child's year group and is kept in the same alphabetical index files. Inside the folders are kept the unstapled sheets containing the general factual information, a new language development sheet (which I shall expand on later), the number progress sheet, the teacher's comment page and an updated teacher's and other person's signature sheet. The locally produced Surrey Pupils Record Card is also placed in this folder. We did not feel it appropriate to include a behaviour profile of each pupil, but reserved copies of this chart for use when we felt it was necessary. These profiles have proved to be more adaptable than the previous version. It is easier to add and to discard information: for example, each year we add a pupil's drawing of himself and his family to the file and intend, in most cases, to discard this before the child moves on to Middle School. We find that medical and psychological reports are also easier to insert and extract from the file. As a result we have found as teachers that the very adaptability of our profile has enabled our system of recording to grow in keeping with the increasing depth of parent involvement and the needs of our pupils.

Pupil involvement

At present, we involve our pupils in two main aspects of their records.
A   They are encouraged from the very early stages to take part in the formation of their school notes. We use a multi-method approach system of language development which includes the testing of pupils at the end of each specified level of development. Although each member of staff has experience in administering these tests, for various reasons it falls to me to carry out the bulk of the testing. When a teacher feels that a group of pupils has mastered the skills taught by a specific level, the children come to me for their tests. They help to prepare the few necessary arrangements for the activity such as finding books and a reasonably private place to work. I have a quiet room, comfortably furnished with carpet, low table and several easy chairs. No major changes are made in the layout of the room and the children may sit or lie in whichever position pleases them, the only condition being that they consider their own privacy and that of the other children.

The actual test is an exciting and enjoyable experience for the children and myself. The emphasis is not on competition but on finding out the skills they have learnt and the areas in which they may need extra practice. As soon as the test booklet is completed, I ask the children whether they would like me to mark the test privately with them or to complete the marking in a group situation. Their choice is not always what one would expect and they have the right to the choice of confidentiality.

Marking consists of transferring the information from the test booklet on to an item analysis and score sheet. Before beginning the marking, I extract the previous test score sheet and the child and I look together to see where we are hoping for improvement. Marking begins: as we do it the reasons for errors are freely discussed and we often have a chuckle together about an amusing sentence. When the item analysis sheet is complete, I ask the pupil if he can see what he has learnt. Several children are perfectly able to see their strengths and have been able to tell me in which skill, if any, they need extra practice. For example, Sandra (aged 6 years) was capable of telling me that she needed more practice on the alphabetical order skills. For other children we take time to look at the sections and discuss whether or not special practice is needed. When a clustering of errors indicates that it is necessary, the pupil and I work out an agreed programme which will give practice in that particular strategy. Sometimes it is not easy to judge between incomplete knowledge of a skill and accidental mistakes and, in those cases where the joint process of marking has not shown the difference, I usually ask the child if he thinks he would benefit from some more practice in that section.

The actual physical experience of seeing what is needed has a value of its own; the child is in no doubt as to what areas show strength and weakness and even where a practice programme is not planned, I mention that as they know of a possible weakness they can be more careful in this aspect on the next level. For example, Mary (aged 6 years) and I found that her only mistakes were made at the ends of each of the longer sections of the test. When I asked whether she knew why this was so, she readily volunteered that she 'might have been a bit tired' at these places. Although by agreement we did not devise a special programme, Mary had learnt to sustain careful concentration by the next test.

After the pupil and I have 'read' the test results, we look together at the previous tests once more and assess what progress has been made. The item analysis sheets are stapled beneath one duplicated sheet which contains spaces for my comment, brief notes of planned practice areas and a section for pupil and parent statements at each level. When I have written my notes, I read them to the pupil, explaining what they say and usually asking if it is a fair statement. After filling in the practice strategies, I indicate the section for personal recording and inquire whether the pupil would like to make a comment about the way he feels about the test. I offer to write the words and also ensure that the child understands that a remark about oneself does not have to be made. Once again the responses are not what one would readily expect: the majority of children do make comments. Quite a number of them keep their statements to a brief sentence such as *I liked it* or *I feel all right about it* but there are some pupils who have more to say. When Alan (aged 5 years) was tested at the end of the first level, he had his dictation on the tip of his tongue: *I liked my test and I am happy about it.* The depth of feeling in his voice and his proud bearing at that moment were most striking. Rachel (aged 7 years) had six errors from a maximum score of fifty on her test. She thought very deeply about her personal comment and asked me to write: *I like it very much doing tests and I am not very sad because I just had a few wrong.*

As with Rachel, most statements do not spring readily to the lips. Sally (aged 6 years) wanted to make a personal note but was having difficulty finding the words so we agreed to score Adam's test to give Sally some time to think. As both pupils had opted to have their tests marked together, Adam (aged 6 years) was in the room. Without any preconceived motive, I turned to Adam and asked if he thought he would find it easy to make a statement. Adam replied, *I don't think it will be easy but I think I will make a comment.* I find this a remarkably perceptive statement for a 6 year old to make. Whatever one's age, it is never an easy task to make a self-critical judgement about one's work.

Although it is a matter of personal judgement, I believe pupil statements are basically honest. Where pupils learn from the test their achievement falls short of their expectation, they may decline to comment, yet there are a few who wanted to have their disappointment noted. The professional morality of asking a child in this position to make a personal comment is brought into focus. It must be emphasised that the child has a choice of whether or not to make a comment. His right to make this choice unhindered by real or implied pressure is where the crux of the professional question lies. Indeed any open form of assessment allows the person examined to make a judgement on himself. To be able to discuss the result of the test and the feelings involved in a correspondingly open atmosphere can only help a person to grow in maturity. The cooperative marking and the jointly planned strategies for improvement overcome any possible decline in confidence and the content of the conversation about the test underlines the constructive nature of the activity.

B   The other means of involving children in their own records begins during the marking of the language tests. Although it does not depend on the language programme, I find that the comparative quiet, privacy and often one-to-one relationship of the marking time gives me the opportunity I need for introducing this second level of involvement. During the marking, I have to extract the language sheet from the pupil's complete record. When I am replacing it in the folder, I casually leaf through some pages saying to the pupil that this is his school record. I might mention that it tells how his 'number work is coming along' and without undue emphasis, I may add, for example, 'on this page, the teachers who have taught you at this school have written about the way you were working'. I continue by saying that if the child would like me to go through his record and read the teachers' comments to him, I would be pleased to do it; all he has to do is ask. I also add that I will only read it to him privately. Once again it is a matter for pupil choice.

One of the major fears of adults concerning this aspect of pupil involvement is that, for some reason, it will be a blow to the pupil's confidence. I recall in particular John (aged 6 years) to whom I read his teachers' comments. Most of the paragraphs noted that John seemed content in his own company. At nursery stage he went through extended periods of solitary, parallel and eventually associative play. I asked him in simple terms if he remembered whether this was so and he replied affirmatively. All his teachers noted his rather quiet, retiring manner and his undoubted academic potential. On the very latest statement, his present teacher had noted that John was 'a very pleasant member of the class'. As I finished reading, John leant back in the easy chair with a certain air of contentment and a rapturous smile on his face. This particular example illustrates that the process can be emotionally enriching. A pupil has the opportunity to see himself through the eyes of others. How often do adults have this chance? If and when they do, it usually comes in the destructive context of a caustic comment or sarcastic phrase overheard. Our fears as adults can cloud the issues involved in this aspect of pupil involvement. Inner security grows from the development of an honest and healthy self-image. I firmly believe that it is part of our professional duty as educators to accord our pupils this opportunity.

As a staff we are considering developing this aspect of pupil involvement. At the moment the process is one-sided, for the pupil does not always, at first school level, have the necessary basic skills to make his own personal record about his school life in general. Foremost in our consideration is the possibility of using taped pupil statements which are later transcribed and inserted into the whole document. We feel that this development will add a new dimension to our pupil records.

Access

Parents of the pupils at our school are involved in the school record on their child from the beginning. When a child is to enter our nursery class, several informal visits are arranged for the new pupil and his family so that he may begin to become accustomed to his future school surroundings. Consequently he is more confident on starting school and this enables me to have a relatively relaxed conversation with his parents. In a quiet corner of the nursery room where some coffee-making facilities are laid on, I begin to fill in the admission register. When this is complete, I pick up a fresh record folder and explain to the parents that this will be their child's school record folder. I show them the empty language, number and teacher comment sheets and say that they may see this record again when their child has completed a language test or indeed, whenever they might request it. I mention that, should they wish to note down information about their child, we can also add a parents' sheet to the record. With the parents' help, I fill in the frontispiece of factual detail. Although it is a repetition of almost the same data as were entered in the admission register, it is a valuable exercise to engage in at that particular time, for often, when I have finished writing, the parent may say, for example, that they are somewhat anxious because their child is left-handed or suffers from slight asthma. I ask if they would like to note it in the record. This they do on what was intended to be the teachers' page, for I add that another page can easily be inserted. Thus it is that in several instances the parent has made a contribution to a pupil's record before the teacher has seen the document.

When the staff discussed the possibility of parental access to pupil notes I found that we were united in the view that the content of a school record is as much the concern of the parent and pupil as of the teacher. It surprised us to read in the National Foundation for Educational Research *Newsletter* 1977 on the Schools Council Record-Keeping in Primary Schools Project that there are some educationists who feel that school records are solely a form of communication between teachers and as such are a necessary part of professionalism. Not one of our teachers made patronising remarks about parents not being able to understand the notes. One member of staff said that she had considered the possibility of parental access when writing statements on pupils over the previous two to three years. I strongly believe that for teachers to grow in professionalism they must be accorded the dignity of trust and this is especially so regarding the diplomacy needed to keep honest and fair records about a child.

What did cause the staff some concern was the fact that a few pupils have reports sent to us by the educational psychologist. The question arose as to whether we would in effect be keeping a dual set of records if we placed these separately to the profile. Inasmuch as it is neither ethical nor possible for a member of one profession to justify the statements of a member of another profession, we felt that these reports should remain private and be extracted from the main folder. The position with case conference reports is similar, in that they contain the views of persons outside the school. We also agreed that the same confidentiality should be accorded to the previous school record of a child who has transferred to our school. However, we did not think that this extraction should be done secretly, but that the parents should know of it and of the reasons for removing such documents.

The staff were also concerned about whether they should use the profiles during the formal parent interviews or open evenings. We jointly decided against this for several reasons. One of the primary factors was that we felt a 'one person distance' was necessary. Teachers are emotionally involved with their class groups and, although it was felt to be a remote possibility, an occasion might arise when disagreement on the content of a file could occur. In these cases, the more objective viewpoint of the head teacher would be helpful. Equally important is the time factor. It is an unfortunate fact that at parent and teacher meetings there is often less than five minutes' time for a child's progress to be discussed. To be able to talk with the teacher and look at a whole profile in five minutes or less was not thought possible. We wished the parents to have a calm and unhurried atmosphere to study their child's notes. Yet another reason for not using profiles on these occasions was that we would be obliged to use them all. As teachers we did not feel it our duty to put pressure, albeit implied pressure, upon parents to read the profiles. We recognised that not everyone wanted to see their child in print through other people's eyes. As with pupils, it had to be a matter for the parents' choice.

To inform the parents of our decision to 'open' records, I made a brief note in the school newsletter that we were working towards such a system. The subsequent newsletter contained this paragraph:

School Records
You may have seen a lot of writing in the press recently about 'secret' records on school children. Do you remember my mentioning in the last term's 'In Touch' how we were working towards a system whereby a child's record would be open to his/her parents? Well, over recent weeks, usually linked with the end of level Scott Foresman tests, parents have been able to see their child's notes. Several parents have themselves commented on or added information to the record. If you would like to see your child's record, please pop in to see me – if I'm busy then we can arrange a later date.

It is an interesting fact that, as a result of the above paragraph, I only had one reasonably immediate request to see a pupil record. It was from a parent whose child had begun in the nursery class just one month earlier.

Apart from the factual information sheet which I had written in her presence, the record was bare!

We invite parents to contribute to their child's notes. On the language programme sheet to which the score sheets are stapled, there is a space for the pupils and parents to comment. In the privacy of my room, I explain the information gained by the test to the parent who has taken up the invitation to see what has been learnt. After having done so, I suggest that the parent might want to study it at greater length. I indicate the parent comment section and provide a pen 'just in case' they should want to make a comment. (Needless to say that if they do make a remark here, the child enjoys knowing what his parent's opinions were when he arrives for his next language test.) Before finally leaving them to peruse the language section of the notes, I remark that I shall leave their child's school records on the low table should they wish to look through them. I also provide an extra sheet of blank paper if they have not already begun a parents' page commenting that they might have relevant information which they would want to add to the profile. Assuring them that I shall try to answer any queries they may have, I move to the far end of my room ostensibly to continue with my work but, in reality, to give them some degree of privacy to study the record. Parent comments range from statements such as 'Excellent work' or 'I am pleased at the way he has settled down to the work' to longer, involved and very perceptive notes about a child's behaviour at home. For example, William's mother wrote (quoted with her permission):

William seems to have picked up interest in reading on own at home as well as making a sudden improvement in school. He has started reading on his own without having to be prompted. However, he is not at all interested in writing at home and when he does write, will take a long time. I think that his friend's absence from school has been fortunate for him in the fact that he has been forced to make other friends and this has given him more confidence. It has also given him a chance to concentrate better on his lessons.

I am very pleased with his progress over the last few months.

(Signed by mother.)

September
I am pleased William has done well in comprehension and especially in alphabetical order which is his weak point. I am surprised he doesn't seem to understand the part on positions, but this is something he is bound to grasp as he grows older. He enjoys doing the tests because I asked him myself at home.

(Signed by mother.)

One or two parents have taken the blank page home to write down their comments. Without exception our parents are appreciative of the opportunity for involvement in their child's personal record. It is interesting that the National Foundation for Educational Research noted that only 55 per cent of their sample schools provided parents with written documentation about their children. I believe that we use our pupil profiles in a way which is even more constructive than the school reports which they seem to imply are educationally good practice. Not only can all our parents have the tests explained to them and have the opportunity to read a considered report on their child's progress but they can also become involved themselves by their contribution to this record. This profile is therefore a vital, worthwhile working document with parents, pupils and teachers working associatively for the educational well-being of the child.

Among the advantages that access to our profiles can hold is one that stems from their continuity as a record. They can be drawn upon when a pupil is having some social, emotional or academic difficulty. When a teacher is anxious about a pupil's development, we try to arrange a meeting with the parents either in school or at their home, where we can discuss our concern about the child. It helps us all to be able to use the profiles freely and openly on these occasions.

Implications for the future

Access to school records is only a part of our openness as a school. We do our best to keep parents informed of all our activities and of interesting items or changes in the school organisation. This is achieved through posters on the parents' noticeboard and also through the twice- or sometimes thrice-termly newsletter which is circulated to parents, friends and pre-school families. Much work has been done over recent years to encourage the parents' confidence with regard to educational matters. There is a degree of social fragmentation in the school's locality and in the past there has been a general air of dependence upon decision makers who mostly live outside the area. With an impending age of participation close at hand and in the absence of any other significant social crossover point, it seemed the natural thing to try to develop the confidence of parents and their ability to influence constructively decisions about their environment. Such a motive on the school's part can be construed as a variation on a reconstructionist theme, whereby the school becomes an agent of social change in terms of its effect upon parents. The encouragement of involvement in their child's school record plays a part in developing a greater awareness of educational matters in parents who may often be too shy, hesitant or embarrassed to ask pertinent questions.

Amongst the advantages the interpersonal contact over records holds for me in this respect is that it presents an opportunity for holding an openly education-based discussion with parents who might not normally attend curriculum-based Parent and Teacher Association gatherings. The depth of their interest and desire for involvement in school affairs is illustrated by their latest project. They have undertaken to design and produce a printed booklet of information about our school. It is important as a landmark, for it is the beginning of true parental decision-making about the school. With the style of parent–teacher relationships we have and the tremendous parent support we as teachers feel, it seems right to us to bring our parents more into the organisation of the school.

Our staff decision to 'open' the pupil records is part of a larger process of growth. As with parents, teachers also need to be prepared for what the future will ask of them. As heads we are asked to consult staff on many issues and, if such consultation is to be a meaningful experience, the teachers need to have developed an extended professional perspective. Opportunity has to be found for them to exercise their capacity for making increasingly important decisions about the whole complex organisation which is the school. This professional growth does not happen overnight nor by magic; it needs positive nurturing. The discussions we have had over recent years as a staff concerning pupil records have had a part in our growth. The decisions on records which have been made show the growing capacity of the staff to partake in responsible decision-making. The development of this capacity in all areas, including records, has contributed to and encouraged the teachers' confidence in their professionalism to the extent that they no longer feel the need to maintain unquestioningly the mystique and secrecy associated with the professional ethic. Their current discussion concerns the possibility of parents observing our formal staff meetings as an initial step towards parental participation in what may eventually become a form of school 'gathering' or 'council'. In such a mature decision-making context, therefore, it is not surprising that the staff discussion on parental access to pupil records was based on rational and constructive argument. As a staff we are now confident enough in our professional abilities not to need the bolster of secrecy in such areas as records any longer. We concluded that confidential records had become inappropriate when pupil, parent and teacher relationships were based on friendliness, honesty and trust in professionalism.

The all-round development of the pupil forms the focus of our efforts in creating and adapting our system of records. The documents are used to encourage a healthy self-image in the child. We believe it is as important for children to appreciate their abilities as it is for them to recognise, in a constructive context, the aspects of their work or behaviour which need practice or adjustment. It is equally valuable for children to know that the adults who care about them are aware of their talents. From our experience with records in particular, we have learnt that a child is capable of constructive self-criticism at a very early age. If this capacity can be harnessed it can bring benefits to the pupil which will remain with him throughout his school career and possibly into adulthood.

Whilst this has been an account of the system we have evolved in a first school, there may be aspects of it which could be adapted to the later stages of education. I believe that the education system as a whole is poised to achieve tremendous advances over the next half-century. With adaptability as the keynote in such areas as learning styles, teaching time and school organisation, a need will be created for correspondingly flexible pupil record systems. Schools at all levels will need to prepare for change. The developments we have begun at our school have already rewarded us richly as pupils, parents and teachers. On the strength of our experience, and without any hesitation, I can commend the extending of involvement in school records. In our school it has become a source of increasing support and pleasure.

11   Higher education:
School for Independent Study

JOHN STEPHENSON

On the DipHE programme in the School for Independent Study at North East London Polytechnic, we have dispensed with pre-arranged syllabuses and externally imposed assessments and have for the past four years made exclusive use of student's own Statements. These Statements cover students' own self-assessment of interests, abilities and achievements at the outset; their long-term aspirations and more immediate educational goals; their detailed plans for learning; and the details of their terminal assessment. So far, approximately four hundred students have completed their Statements and just under half of that number have completed their programmes of study. This paper sets out our reasons for doing this, how we do it and explores some of its wider implications.

Our purpose is to provide students with an educational experience which enables them to be generally competent and independent. By this we mean that they should be capable of coping with a wide variety of different situations, many of them unfamiliar, without being dependent upon the direction of others. We are convinced of the relevance of this by our observations of the nature of society and the needs of individuals within it. Many of the traditional props, such as the extended family, and the Church, are less important than in the past. The skills and aptitudes demanded by jobs are changing, with retraining and constant change of practice becoming the normal experience. There is considerable mobility, bringing young people into new and different social environments. It is increasingly difficult to make accurate predictions of job requirements more than a few years ahead. (Manpower planning is becoming increasingly a speculative activity.) Social practices, moral codes and personal relationships are much more flexible, with more onus being placed on the individual to determine his own code of practice. In short, change is becoming normal, and the capacity to cope with and participate in change is increasingly at a premium.

We are further encouraged by our view of the nature of knowledge itself. It is clear that what is known is constantly being extended, refuted or disregarded. What it was essential to know in a given situation ten years ago is very often not essential now. New or different knowledge is constantly being applied to the same situation in response to people's greater understanding of that situation, their changing perception of it, and the greater volume of possible relevant knowledge from which to choose. What were previously held to be fundamental truths are often no longer assumed to be so. Current fundamental truths will themselves in turn be discarded, replaced or refined. In other words, the identification of a given body of knowledge as essential for any educated person to have is increasingly becoming a difficult and even futile task. In its place, the ability to learn, challenge and extend knowledge is much more useful.

Thirdly, we have been influenced by our view of the nature of learning and the ways in which knowledge is extended. At its simplest level we believe in learning by doing, which in this case means directly involving the student in his own learning process. We believe that trial and error is a natural and effective method of learning, involving, as it does, an original tentative shot at setting out the nature of a problem and a possible solution; having a go to see if it works; and, in the light of its failure, producing a more sophisticated statement of the nature of the problem. People who are competent at learning in this way are most likely to be capable of coping with changing circumstances, without dependence upon others to show the way.

Fourthly, we were conscious of a feeling that many students pursuing courses of higher education were doing so largely because of the social and economic pressure on them to gain the highest level of qualification of which they were capable. In many cases this meant shopping around to find the course or college most likely to take them. Even when a happy marriage is arranged whereby the student gets into a generally relevant field or subject there are problems. For instance, course planners' assumptions about the general level at which all freshers must begin inevitably frustrate all but the predictable student. Syllabuses include items which relate more to the interests of staff or the range of expertise available in the department than to the actual needs or interests of the student. Little if any effort is made to diagnose which skills and knowledge the student brings with him. Neither are the specific requirements implied by the student's own aspirations for his life after he's finished formal education, taken into account. In short, there is often a severe mismatch between what is provided and what is needed, of a kind which would be laughably tragic were it to be found within the legal or medical services. Imagine the outcry if a patient went to a clinic wishing to be made fit and well and the doctors gave him laxatives without bothering to discover that what was really required was a repair to a broken leg. No doubt such doctors could refer to the fact that in their experience many previous groups of patients had benefited from laxatives and that in their general opinion a well-functioning bowel system is a highly desirable thing to have. What's more, they are expert at giving laxatives.

Finally, we wished to give more recognition to the importance of the affective domain in education. The ability to cope with the unfamiliar is as much dependent upon self-confidence as it is on problem solving and other related skills. Our own observations, matched by those of the employers who were consulted, were that many school leavers lacked purpose and confidence – they did not know what they were about, or did not have what the Polytechnic's Director once described as 'the necessary arrogance'. We believed that a process of self-analysis supported by tutorial and peer group guidance would help to stimulate purposeful personal development, and that the achievement of personally set goals would lead to the development of self-confidence. If such achievement is further applauded by the real world and the educational establishment, then self-confidence is substantial and assured.

For all these reasons, argued at greater length in the documents setting out the DipHE programme, we deliberately confront each student with his new, unfamiliar situation, namely his own education for the next two years. We require him to formulate his own educational problem, devise his own solution to that problem, implement that solution, and, at the end, test and demonstrate the extent to which it is successful. We have rejected the opposite and traditional practice of learned and external bodies arrogantly determining the educational problem of others (usually in large bundles), imposing their own mass solutions (called syllabuses), and applying a common test of achievement. This is nearly always done on a knowledge rather than skill basis. Such approaches as these deny students their own valuable learning experience.

We recognise the advantages of the existing system of externally imposed syllabuses and assessments in establishing public confidence. Not only do the public in general and employers in particular need to be satisfied that the end product of education has a warranty of quality backed by the collective authority of the educational establishment, but also the student himself needs some external criticism and recognition of the value of what he proposes to do and what he achieves. Where inexperienced non-expert students are trusted with tasks normally assigned only to established academics, public recognition is not only desirable, it is absolutely essential. The importance of the Statement to our work is that it is the main vehicle for requiring students to make public and explicit the rationale for, and details of, their proposed programmes, thus exposing them to rigorous public criticism. If they survive this process then recognition can follow quite readily.

What the Statement consists of

The Statement consists of an agreement between the student, the

Polytechnic, and his tutor, that a particular programme of study is both valid and feasible and if completed would be worthy of the award of a CNAA DipHE. The formal part of the agreement is as follows:

APPENDIX A
Experience
I present here a review of my past educational and relevant life experience.

APPENDIX B
Present Position
At present I am able to identify that I possess the following capacities (intellectual and practical skills), strengths and weaknesses relevant to the pursuit of my programme of work.

APPENDIX C
Outline Future Planning
I am able to state, at present, the following future plans, personal, academic and vocational, on gaining the Diploma.

APPENDIX D
Skills, Knowledge and Qualities Needed
In order to realise my future plans I am at present able to identify that by the end of my programme of study I will need to have acquired the following intellectual and practical skills, areas of experience and knowledge.

APPENDIX E
Proposed Programme of Study
In order to achieve the skills, knowledge and experience presented in Appendix D, I have formulated the following plans in the areas of individual, group and other work.

APPENDIX F
Assessment
In order to demonstrate that I have achieved my targets I propose that my individual and group work should be assessed as follows.

Attached to the formal agreement are the six Appendices A to F prepared by the student himself. What follows is an example of one such Statement produced in 1978 by a full-time student after one term's experience. It is quoted in full, not because it is thought to be typical or good, but because it illustrates very well what is meant by the various Appendices.

APPENDIX A
Educational Experience
1959–64:
   Attended six years of primary schooling and graduated with Grade 1 Primary School Certificate

1965–9:

Attended five years of Secondary Schooling and securing two O levels in English Literature and Needlework

1970–71:

Attended Secretarial School and obtaining Pitman's Certificate in Typewriting and Shorthand

Other Relevant Experience

1972:

Worked as a secretary to the directoress of a modeling agency

1973:

Worked as a clerk in a large textile factory

1974–5:

Attended State Enrolled Nurses' training securing a State Enrolled Nurses' Diploma

1976–7:

Worked as a State Enrolled Nurse at Plaistow Maternity Hospital

A very varied background beginning with an involved experience in school. Was associated with a variety of clubs and societies, both academic and recreational. I was an active member of the Red Cross Society and the School Literary, Debating and Dramatic Society. Participated in a number of inter-school debates and school plays. Through this experience I gained a lot of confidence in public speaking and working with other members of the club.

After leaving school I went into Secretarial School because that's what my parents wanted me to do. After a year's training I worked as a secretary for a year and had to leave because the agency was closing down. Then I worked as a clerk for about a year in a large textile factory. My experience in both jobs have made me familiar with office routine and internal politics of large, private and public enterprises.

I went into nursing to get away from the daily office routine. Having worked as a nurse for more than four years, I have come in contact with people at all levels from patients to staff. A nurse, besides performing nursing duties has to reckon with the emotions, attitudes and problems of her patients. During emergencies and daily nursing routine we work as a team with colleagues, the medical, administrative and other hospital staff.

My reason for leaving nursing is because for a long time I have had a desire to pursue a course of higher education. This desire is the course of a few reasons. First being that it would enable me both to improve my standing in society and at the same time make a more worthy contribution to the community that I live in. Another reason being that I would like to improve myself and I feel that the challenge of a course in higher education would be a very appropriate way to go about doing it. This way, I feel that I am not just self-indulging in a par-ticular fashion but also having a tangible and beneficial effect in society and myself.

I feel that I am a credible person now at twenty-five years of age, for pursuing a high education course specially my specialist subject which is Information

Processing. I feel that studying this subject would stretch my capabilities which until today have not been done so to the fullest.

I have also travelled quite widely in and around South East Asia and Europe. This experience has made me a more self-confident and independent person.

APPENDIX B
Present Position
Looking at the resumé outlined in Appendix A, I feel that I do possess certain skills and capacities which I acquired more as an accidental by-product of my past educational and job experience.

I can, however, identify certain skills that I now possess. They are:

i Typewriting
Intermediate Stage Gross speed – 40 words per min. Accuracy: 100 per cent

ii Report Writing
Only as far as my past education and jobs have required and allowed to exercise this skill.

iii Oral Capabilities
I can in most instances make myself be understood and I don't have any difficulties understanding anyone.

iv Languages
Can speak five languages–English, Malay, Punjabi, Hindi and Hokkien (a Chinese dialect). Written knowledge of English, Malay and Punjabi.

v Organising
I am fairly competent in this skill as I was responsible for the running of a ward in a hospital.

The one weakness that stands out like a sore thumb, is a tendency to put things off to the last minute in particular working on a given assignment, but I'm always capable of meeting deadlines.

APPENDIX C
Outline Future Planning
After gaining the Diploma, I hope to go on to attain a Degree and then do postgraduate work in Information Studies, especially in the use of computers for Information Processing as applied to libraries.

Hopefully I would like to get a BA by Independent Studies at North East London Polytechnic or a place at any of the colleges which offer degree courses for Information Studies.

I do not have definite vocational plans as this will depend on the work I do in the next few years but I can envisage working in one of the following fields of employment.

Government Departments: Many departments have information services for the use of their staff and public usage e.g. Foreign and Commonwealth Office, Ministry of Agriculture, Fisheries and Food, Department of Industry, Department of Health and Social Security and The Public Records Office

Academic: Universities, Polytechnics and Technical Colleges, National and Scientific Libraries

Industry: Manufacturing, Technical, Commercial, Financial establishment.

138   Progress Towards a Solution

APPENDIX D
Skills, Knowledge and Qualities Needed

Individual Work
1 The ability to demonstrate a knowledge of program skills and program techniques relevant to my area of studies.
2 The ability to demonstrate documentation skills
3 Acquire File Handling Techniques
4 A fluency in Cobol programming language

Group Work
Acquire Diagnostic Skills
The ability to
1 Locate and collect data and information
2 Assimilate data selectively, modify and adapt data to new problem areas
3 Identify real life problems and operations and make keen observational analysis of these situations
4 To collaborate with others in the group in organising, researching and developing projects and putting them into operation, within constraints of time and resource

APPENDIX E
Proposed Programme of Study

Individual Work
Methods of Study
1 Tutorial
Through weekly tutorials with my Individual Work Tutor in which I will discuss my project work
2 Lectures
Through attending lectures in Faculty of Business Studies every Monday and Friday
3 Projects
Through project work in the use of Computer Systems

1st Year
Terms 2 and 3
1 *OBJECTIVES*
a. To be able to identify problems solveable by a computer and those that are not
b. To become aware of computer peripherals e.g. Line Printer, Card-Reader, Teletype
2 *AREAS OF STUDY*
a. To use data and program operation equipments
b. To become familiar with the COBOL programming
c. A knowledge of program techniques
d. A knowledge of file structure
e. Attend lectures on Advanced Programming. Syllabus: Linear Lists, Arrays,

Trees Structures, File Organisation, Data Structure Handling, Languages and Grammars, Compilers.

3   *ASSIGNMENTS TO BE COMPLETED*

a. To run a number of elementary programs using COBOL – by the end of term 2

b. To complete a basic Retrieval project on the implement of a system based upon the journals holding of NELP – by end of term 3

2nd Year

A system for the 2nd year cannot at this stage be specified in detail as it is not yet known what systems will be available within NELP.

The program will however be moulded in the following format.

Terms 1 and 2

1   *AREAS OF STUDY*

a. A detailed study of one or two particular Retrieval systems, possibly the MARC (Machine Readable Catalogue) and BLAISE (British Library Automation Information System).

b. Attend lectures on Information Storage and Retrieval.

Syllabus: File Organisation, Sorting and Searching Database Techniques, Virtual Storage Techniques.

2   *ASSIGNMENTS TO BE COMPLETED*

a. Essay on Information Storage and Retrieval. Length: Approx. 2000 words – by end of term 1.

b. Exercises in the use of one or both of the MARC or BLAISE Systems and if possible assist in a live situation, e.g. write or implement some software relevant to the system – by end of term 2.

Term 3

Document and consolidate studies, i.e. write dissertation and present documentation of program systems produced.

I append a booklist as an indication of the basic reading I will be pursuing, although I will expand the booklist in the course of my study.

Group Work

I will follow the project program of the school and will contribute Individual Reports on the projects which will describe and analyse:–

a. Individual contribution to the group project

b. How specific skills were used during the project

Reading List

Watters, *Cobol Programming*

Farini, *Cobol Simplified*

Saxon, *Cobol – A Self-Instructional Manual*

Parkin, *Cobol for students*

Davis & Litecky, *Elementary Cobol Programming*

ICL Pub. *Introduction to ICL Cobol*

Fry, *Computer Appreciation*

Henley, *Computer based library and Information Systems*

Houghton, *Computer based Information Retrieval Systems*

Lancaster, *Information Retrieval On-Line*
Vickery, *Information Retrieval*
Jones, *Classification for Information Retrieval*
Becker & Hayes, *Information Storage and Retrieval*
Langefors, *Information Systems Architecture*
Heilinger, *P. B. Library Automation: Experience Methodology, and Technology of the Library as an Information system*
Cox & Grose *Organisation and Handling of bibliographic records by computer*
Sanderson *Management Information Systems and The Computer*
Davies *Computer Cataloguing System*

APPENDIX F
Methods of Assessment
I will submit as evidence of my work achieved throughout the program, my final individual product which will be
a. Dissertation on the nature and size of the program of Information Retrieval. General review of modern methods and techniques.
Length: approx. 7000 words
b. *Projects*
1st Year: Journal listing system of NELP
2nd Year: Software enhancement for MARC system and exercises in Information Retrieval using BLAISE. Subject to these being the systems available at NELP
These will demonstrate the skills listed in relation to Individual Work in Appendix D
   My work will be assessed by my tutor and assessors who are competent in this field.

Group Work
This will be assessed by my ability to use basic diagnostic skills listed in Appendix D and I will use the opportunity to discuss my knowledge and employment of these skills with my individual report in the set situation.

The Statement has three main components. First, Appendices A, B, and C represent the formulation of the student's educational problem as perceived by himself; secondly D and E represent the proposed detailed educational solution to the problem; and finally Appendix F represents the basis on which the appropriateness of the solution is tested. These three components roughly correspond with the various phases of the DipHE programme and what follows is a brief description of how they are produced.

The formulation of the educational problem (A, B, C)

This takes place in the first three or four weeks of the programme. During this period the student is with a group of fifteen peers with a personal tutor. Each appendix is written in sequence and preparation for each lasts about a week. For Appendix A the problem is to encourage the student to open up about himself and for him to feel sufficiently secure to be able to do so. Much use is made of team building exercises to boost the support from peers in which the tutor is expected to join. Students are encouraged not only to write down their personal histories, focusing on what seems to them to be most important, but also to exchange their writings with their colleagues and tutors who do not reject or denigrate anything which is written or said but give their reactions to it. As often as not, this process of mutual exchange of experiences and reactions leads to a more thoughtful and penetrating personal history by the end of the week. Students are able to compare their own lot with that of others and very quickly find themselves talking at great length about themselves and in return asking searching questions of their fellows. The group of fifteen frequently breaks down to sets of four to six for this activity so that a variety of experiences and reactions is encountered. At intervals during this week the School provides specific inputs such as seminars on the aims of education, the wider context of the DipHE in Higher Education, and the factors which contribute to success or failure in school. There is discussion, in particular, on the value of planning educational experiences and the importance of starting with the student rather than the subject. Wherever possible the activities are made enjoyable and everyone is made conscious of the need to support each other. There is no rigid timetable of activities, except on the few occasions when an input is required for the whole year group (e.g. an introduction to the staff of the Polytechnic's counselling services), which means that groups operate rather like an infant class where the class teacher has the freedom to switch activities to suit the moods and changing needs of the group.

Appendix B is a more analytical version of A, where the student is encouraged to set out his strengths and weaknesses. This is particularly difficult and students find themselves constantly adding to their personal inventories. The pattern of provision is as before, with the addition of self-evaluation exercises. Tests of specific skills, such as literacy and numeracy, are available but for other less obvious skills group exercises leading to mutual evaluation are used. Access to the Polytechnic's counselling tutors and other specialists is arranged as required. Inevitably there is constant reference back to Appendix A which continues to develop during this phase.

For Appendix C, access to careers advisers and ideally to specialists in the chosen field is very important. Students are encouraged not only to indicate likely destinations but also to explore the implications of getting there. For instance, a student wishing to become a teacher would need to know the requirements for gaining recognition, the different ways in which it can be achieved, some indication of his preferred route, and to show some understanding of the place his DipHE would have in it. Again, discussions in sets are very useful in helping students to come to terms with what they want to do. For many of them it is the first time they have ever been required to think seriously about the future. It is quite legitimate for students to remain doubtful about their preferences, provided they are clear about their doubt and that it is expressed in such a way as to form a useful basis for educational planning. An example would be 'I wish to work with adolescents but I wish to keep open the options of probation work, teaching, or youth and community work. The implication of keeping these options open are that my Diploma programme should contain . . . .' Students are then required to indicate a first tentative solution to the problem they are setting for themselves. In one brief paragraph they set out the general lines of their proposed programme of study and then submit their total Interim Statement, as it is called, to external criticism and validation.

Preparing the solution (D and E)

Once the Interim Statement is approved (see later for details of the Validating Board) the student can proceed to plan his programme, knowing that he is generally on the right lines. Clearly, detailed planning can only take place on the basis of experience in the chosen areas, so this phase of the course, lasting four months, consists of various placements and workshop activities. For instance, the potential teacher of deaf children would be introduced to those Polytechnic staff who share the same interest and who have appropriate experience and expertise. Preliminary background work is begun, schools for the deaf are visited, practising teachers in the field are interviewed, and arising from all those discussions, observations, self-assessments of specific abilities, and nego-tiations, the student is able to state with confidence those learning outcomes it would be most helpful for him to achieve (Appendix D) and the most appropriate ways of achieving them (Appendix E). The student's own specialist tutor is crucial in this activity, acting as adviser, critic, assessor and source of information and contacts. The contract between them not only spells out the content of the programme, but also indicates the learning methods, frequency of tutorial contacts, types and amount of assignments to be completed, and location and duration of field placements.

Completion of the programme(F)

When the Final Statement is validated, and the programme implemented as planned, the student is required to present for assessment precisely what he set out to present. He is kept to what he set for himself in Appendix D and the means of assessment stated in F. Aimless wandering from his own purpose-built syllabus is therefore not encouraged and is unlikely to lead to success. The questions asked by the Assessment Board are, 'Has this student achieved what is set out in Appendix D in the manner indicated in Appendix F?' and secondly, 'Has he done so at a level comparable to that which would be expected of an undergraduate completing his second year of his Honours Degree course?' If 'yes', then a Diploma is awarded. If 'no', then it is not. This is extremely important because the fact that what is put into Appendices D and F is for real means that students take that part of the planning process extremely seriously. It also ensures that the Statement actually does represent an accurate profile of the work done.

Validation of Final Statements

At this stage it is necessary to describe the procedure and criteria used to validate students' Statements and to consider why it is necessary. Initially, all Statements are scrutinised within the School, with a number of tutors, including those not familiar with the student, considering the total package in terms of its cohesion, demand on resources and whether it is likely to lead to the award of the Diploma. In particular the following questions are asked:

Do Appendices A and B provide sufficient evidence of critical self-appraisal?

Is a sense of direction indicated in Appendix C? Is there an awareness in the implications (vocational and academic) of stated intentions?

In Appendix D is there:
– a clear statement of learning objectives which relate to both Individual and Group Work?
– a consistency between these objectives and the goals indicated in Appendix C?
– sufficient emphasis on content (skills/knowledge) especially in terms of Individual Work?
– a clear reference to transferable skills in terms of Group and Individual Work?
– evidence that objectives are sufficiently refined as to be manageable within the context of the programme?
– sufficient regard to coherence and presentation?

In Appendix E is there:
– an overall awareness of the reality of implementing objectives outlined in Appendix D?
– an outline of the substantive elements of Individual Work?
– a clear statement of commitment to a specified output of work within the Individual Work context?
– sufficient indication of the phasing of work in terms of time and emphasis?
– some indication of the nature and frequency of contacts with Special Interest Tutors?

In Appendix F is there:
– a reference to the skills and knowledge (outlined in D) to be demonstrated via Individual Work?
– an indication of the Individual Work product showing sufficient relationship to the above?

When the School's judgement is clear, a sample of the Statements is sent to a panel of people external to the Polytechnic, who meet together and decide whether the School's judgement is appropriate. As a Board they interrogate the School on its judgement and interview all students whose Statements are in some way in doubt, and a range of the rest. Once validated, the Statement represents a commitment by the Polytechnic to resource the programme and, under arrangements agreed with the CNAA, becomes the basis for assessment for the award of DipHE.

Whilst the validated programme is being implemented, students are encouraged by their personal tutors to monitor continually their own progress and the relevance of their programme. It is obvious that throughout the two years of work the student will learn more about his long-term intentions, the detailed implications of his originally stated intentions, the degree of ease or difficulty of different parts of his programme, the relative appropriateness of its various components, and detailed criteria of assessment. To achieve this fine-tuning the student must become accustomed to asking for feedback on his performance and criticism of his programme from both his personal tutor and his specialist tutor. Tutors in their turn must see their role as essentially one of supplying such feedback and criticism in a manner which fosters confidence. Eventually, students learn to exercise their own judgements and to use tutorial and other comments as a means of testing their own judgement of performance rather than the performance itself. To facilitate this process of development, the Validating Board meets each term and can therefore consider proposals for changes more or less as required by the student. It is important to state, however, that the same demands for explicit rationale are made as in the original validation so that changes are deliberate and conscious and not whimsical or uncontrolled drift.

Membership of the Board is made up of individuals who, by their status or achievement, represent success in the outside world. They are not, in the main, the conventional external examiners and this is deliberate policy. At present they consist of an ex Senior Civil Servant, a retired Inspector of Education, a Business Consultant, an Architect, a former Senior Local Government Official, and a Business Executive. We see validation as essentially different from assessment in that a) it represents an important learning experience; b) it provides the opportunity for students to find solutions outside the normal academic solutions; c) it allows students to justify proposals on grounds other than the extent to which they are assessable by conventional means; and d) we are operating a programme designed to help people cope with life outside college and not just with academic work. This last reason is crucial.

Preparation for validation is a formidable task for the student. The Board, to the student, has the same sort of status as a public examinations body and it is therefore taken seriously. A good deal of effort is put into making as explicit as possible the precise nature of the student's educational problem, and the proposed solution, and into communicating the proposal as clearly as possible. The effect of this is that the student is made to be explicit to himself, and to be as clear in his own mind, as he can be about what he wants to do, why he wants to do it, and how he proposes to do it. His commitment to completion of the programme is very high as a consequence. Further, once this revered and august body has validated his statement, the student has the confidence of knowing that what he, as a humble student, is proposing is thought by the establishment to be well worth doing, particularly in terms appropriate to the student himself.

There are also external payoffs of validation. Public confidence in the quality of the proposed programme is guaranteed by this disinterested group of personalities. The Statement itself, suitably endorsed by the Validating Board, and eventually by the DipHE Assessment Board, forms a very useful and informative profile of the student and his work. Potential employers of the student, for instance, will learn more about him from his Statement than by any conventional public certification.

The preparation of Statements has the considerable bonus of being a valuable educational process in itself. Students learn quickly how to communicate effectively both orally and in writing, how to analyse complex situations, how to give and receive critical advice, how to support others in group situations, how to set out a problem, and above all how to negotiate their way around a vast and bureaucratic institution. At the end of this process they understand the difference between long-term educational aims and short-term objectives, and have knowledge of a variety of methods of learning and assessment.

For Assessment, we use the normal established bodies for external assessment of Polytechnic/CNAA sponsored awards. It is very important that we do this in order to establish comparability of standards with other students, to preserve public confidence in the student's achievement, and to give the student marketable credit for his work. To help us do this, there is an Assessment Board constituted on exactly the same basis as Boards for CNAA Degrees, i.e. including external examiners approved by the Council itself. In order to cope with the wide variety of programmes we try to include as full members of the Board an examiner from each of the main activity areas (e.g. the Arts, Natural Sciences etc.). The procedures depend initially, as with CNAA Degrees, on internal assessment by specialist tutors in the appropriate field. In most cases this is the student's own special interest tutor. We also receive a further report from a 'disinterested person', who has not been personally involved with the student but who is competent to judge work at this level in the relevant field. In some cases, particularly where the work is in an obscure or unusual area, written testimonials are solicited, often by the student himself, from established figures in other institutions. External examiners have full access to all produced work, all comments from external assessors and disinterested persons, and can personally interview each student. In practice, all students about whom there is even the slightest doubt are seen, together with a sample of the rest. External examiners read a selection of students' work sent to them in advance (work of their choice), spend about three days in the School meeting with tutors, students and inspecting the total range of work, and attend a final formal meeting to approve the agreed pass list. Afterwards they submit their criticisms and comments to the Polytechnic and the CNAA.

Problems of running such scheme

North East London Polytechnic is no different from any other Polytechnic in that it has a tradition of pre-planned taught courses.

It is therefore of some interest to relate how the innovation came about. It began in 1972 when the Polytechnic was preparing its response to the James Committee's report on Teacher Education and its recommendation that there should be provision for a two year DipHE. A small working party, established under the Chairmanship of the Deputy Director, produced ideas for a new style of course which the Polytechnic decided were worth developing further, and a DipHE Development Unit was set up to make these ideas a reality. The Unit consisted of about a dozen staff working a part of their time each week in detailed specification and preparing the formal submission to the CNAA. They consisted in the main of quite ordinary tutors, in the sense that they were not specialist in the style of work being developed. How could they be, since the work was entirely new?

Their main qualification was that they were interested and were willing to put in the time. They also came from all sections of the Polytechnic. To accommodate the first intake of students, a small School was established consisting in the main of tutors who had been responsible for its development. It should be realised that the Polytechnic has eight major Faculties with about seven hundred academic staff. The School had only six central tutors in 1974 and now has about seventeen. An essential part of its functioning is its contacts with each Faculty, maintained by 'Faculty Linkmen', who are responsible for arranging matches between students and appropriate specialist tutors. These tutors carry on with their normal Faculty-based work and incorporate their DipHE students in ways most convenient to their personal timetables or to the needs of the study. In other words, the whole programme developed within an established system, proved itself to be compatible with it, and has been able to grow.

It is equally important to note that the programme has not demanded more than the normal resource provision for other students in the Polytechnic. For instance, at the time of the School's establishment the whole Polytechnic had a staff–student ratio of under 8 to 1, whilst the School was staffed at 9 or 10 to 1. Today the School's SSR is 10 to 1 which is the target figure for the Polytechnic as a whole. In practice, because each student is 'contracted out' to other Faculties for 0.4 of his time (two days per week) the School needs to allocate about seventeen students to each central-based tutor in order to preserve an overall 10 to 1 SSR. This means that for the preparation of Statements, tutors must deal with classes of seventeen each. To cope with this, students are encouraged to work in small groups or to occupy private study space, whilst individuals have private tutorials. In the Faculties, 0.4 of a student at an SSR of 10 to 1 can command only one twenty-fifth of the specialist tutor's time. The rest is devoted to private study, external placement, attending workshops and lectures, and helping the tutor with his own research activities.

Work of the kind described in this chapter requires a tutor to behave in ways different from normal. He starts by listening to students and proceeds by responding to needs as they become apparent. He has three main roles to play. First, he must build up the student's confidence in himself by recognising that he, the student, has something positive to contribute and by establishing a client/consultant relationship. Secondly, the tutor must continually challenge the student's logic and self-assertions as an aid to increasing his self-awareness, and at the same time give constant feedback on the student's performance. Thirdly, the tutor must be able to respond quickly with appropriate information or learning activities as the needs become apparent. This can be done by the tutor himself or by contracting the student out to colleagues more expert in a particular field. In brief it calls for a considerable shift in the tutor's perception of his role, almost a total reversal. Yet our experience so far has suggested that staff themselves respond very favourably when they are offered the opportunity of moving outside their traditional constraints, and that the most effective agents for staff development are the students themselves.

Another problem is to match specific student needs with specific tutor expertise. So far we have placed over four hundred students without more than a handful being totally unable to find a specialist tutor. It means that instead of producing a fixed timetable in advance, the School must provide agencies for the exchange of information and market places for the arrangement of meetings of students and potential tutors.

There are also implications for the availability of resources. Specialist facilities, provided mainly for other groups of students, need to be available by negotiation to DipHE students. Learning resources should be arranged in resource centres and loaned out on a library basis. These principles are very difficult to establish, particularly when they are currently managed by self-contained discipline-based Departments. Part of the solution depends on the ways in which the institution can compensate the host Department for their use.

It must also be recognised that there are problems for students too. Initially there is a period of disorientation, when previous assumptions about themselves and education are being exposed and questioned. Secondly, there can be frustration if making the right choices proves difficult or the tutors and resources are not readily available. Thirdly, there is a potential for isolation, since there is not a whole group of peers doing exactly the same things and with whom it is possible to exchange information and views and to get some feel of how much relative success is being achieved.

There are also considerable technical difficulties over things like assessment. Normal assessments generally operate on a ranking basis with cut-offs between success and failure rather arbitrarily determined. For rankings to take place a number of students doing comparable work is necessary and this we haven't got. We are therefore forced to assess the actual level of each achievement in isolation and this is extremely difficult particularly with affective skills. Our current solution is to demand from the student explicit Statements of precisely what is to be assessed and to ask academics experienced in examining other undergraduate courses in similar fields to state whether in their opinion what is presented is the sort of thing which a student completing his second undergraduate year might reasonably be expected to do.

We will not, of course, know how successful our use of Statements is for some time yet. We will need to follow up the progress of our Diplomates to see how they fare and of course this we are doing. Our preliminary judgement, based on our own observations of their personal development over the two year period, is that the student benefit is considerable. We have no plans to revert to more traditional methods.

The question that inevitably arises is whether our work is generally applicable to other areas of education. We are convinced that the educational problems to which our work is a tentative solution are general problems, and are present in all institutions of education from primary school to university, and that the educational value of independent study is not constrained by age, level or institutional context. It is also worth noting that those students who appear to have most difficulty with coping with the problem of their own education are those who have transferred directly either from secondary school or from other courses of higher education. Those who come from 'real life' fare much better. We take this to be an indication that educational institutions are not themselves very successful at helping their pupils/students to become more competent.

A further consideration is whether established institutions are capable of adapting themselves in this way. It is important to appreciate in this respect the extent to which North East London Polytechnic is like nearly every other school or college. It has subject departments and faculties, has staff largely with conventional school and college backgrounds, and is constrained educationally by the demands of a publicly established validating body. All that is needed is a small group of committed and energic staff, supported by the Director or Head, who can work out the detailed solutions to the local problems of inertia and tradition. Their solutions, of course, are likely to differ from ours in some respects according to their circumstances and creativity.

12　School and work

CHRISTINA TOWNSEND

This chapter draws attention to the serious difficulties being faced by young people as they attempt to make the transition from school to work. It argues that when designing curricula, teaching methods, assessment and certification, much more account should be taken of the competencies needed for the world of work. It goes on to describe some experimental work, the results of which it is hoped will bridge many gaps dividing the education system, the labour market services, employers and unions. Essentially, the experimental approach is concerned with finding out more about the labour market and what it takes both to get and to hold a job.

Youth unemployment

Most experts seem agreed that within Britain in the immediate forseeable future there is likely to be persistent high unemployment. In this situation, all the evidence[1] suggests that young people attempting to enter the labour market for the first time are at a particular disadvantage. In Britain, unemployment among 16 to 17 year olds rose by 120 per cent between January 1972 and January 1977 compared with a rise of 45 per cent among the working population as a whole. The median duration of unemployment has also increased more rapidly for those aged under 18 than any other group.

Surveys of employers and young people[2] have recently been carried out on behalf of the Manpower Services Commission. Some of the main findings are as follows.

(i)　Most unemployed young people are actively seeking jobs: 40 per cent of those interviewed had applied for more than six jobs and very few had refused an offer of a job.

(ii)　Young people are employed in and recruited for a wide range of jobs for which they are in competition with other age groups. Only in entry to skilled or training jobs do specifically 'young people' jobs exist. For many semi- and unskilled jobs traditionally associated with young people such as clerical, sales, etc., there is increasingly strong competition from older workers, particularly married women.

(iii) About half the employers interviewed believed that the calibre of young people had deteriorated over the past five years in terms of their motivation and basic education. For semi- and unskilled jobs, employers were asked if applicants of broadly similar qualifications were available whether young people or another kind of recruit was preferred. While 42 per cent did not express a preference, 40 per cent preferred housewives returning to work to young people. Even housewives seeking their first job were preferred to young people in the majority of cases when a preference was stated.

(iv) The impact of unemployment is most severe on those young people who have few or no marketable skills or qualifications. In comparison with the better trained and qualified they suffer longer durations of unemployment, are most frequently unemployed, and when employed they tend to work in lower status jobs with poorer prospects of promotion and fewer opportunities for training. This group faces not only increased competition from other age groups, but also increased competition from more able young people who in the present economic climate have to lower their career aspirations.

(v) Many young people were prepared to return to full-time education in order to get a qualification which would help them get a job.

One of the major conclusions resulting from these surveys is that even if an improvement in business activity reduced the general level of unemployment, there might still be a relatively high level of young people unemployed, as many employers would prefer to recruit older, more experienced workers. Further, the number of young people entering the labour market is expected to rise each year until 1981. Total labour market supply is expected to increase from 25.75 million in 1976 to 26.5 million in 1981; partly in consequence of the increase in numbers of young people available for employment, but partly also because of increased participation by married women. The true levels of unemployment for young people over the next few years are likely to be significantly worse than current levels, although the trend upwards will be slowed if unemployment generally should fall.

Given that secondary education is concerned with the preparation of young people for many aspects of adult life besides work, surely the evidence suggests that there is an urgent need for more positive and practical steps to be taken which will help young people with the transition from school to work. The education system can have a significant role in aiding *all to have access* to employment and to compete successfully for employment, even if economic circumstances make it impossible for *all* to be employed *at the same time*.

The aim of the experimental approach to be described is to provide a better understanding of the labour market and what it takes both to get and to hold a job. It is hoped that any new insights will be taken account of when designing curricula, teaching methods, assessment and certification. To avoid any misunderstanding, this is no attempt to 'pervert' the aims of education so as to narrow young people to fit into narrow jobs, but on the contrary to make it more possible for young people to manage their working lives more competently. It is being argued that, even in the final year of secondary school, it is important that any vocational education should be generic and not directed only towards particular types of jobs. This is because, first, the expected job is often not known at the time when the learning experience is provided. Some young people, for example, may be very unclear as to what they want to do and will want to explore further the world of work. Others may have unrealistic career aspirations: they may have romantic ideas about their chosen job and change their minds when meeting reality; they may have abilities which do not meet up with those needed for the work they have chosen; they may have chosen jobs for which there are few vacancies and much competition. The second argument for generic rather than job specific vocational education is the need to help individuals prepare not only for a job but for work characterised by change. Evidence from the population census for Great Britain[3] suggests that it is no longer valid to think in terms of one set of occupational skills being learned once and lasting a lifetime – in *one* year 6.6 per cent of the working population changed occupations, and over half of the changes were major ones. It is being argued, therefore, that vocational education should aim at not only helping a young person to get his or her first job, but to cope with a hazardous and changing labour market. Individuals with more broad-based vocational education and training should be an asset to industry and commerce because of their increased flexibility.

Skills used in the local labour market

It has already been stated that in Britain young people enter a wide range of semi- and unskilled jobs. For those involved with generic rather than job specific vocational education, surely one of the key questions is how they can get to grips with both the diversity and changing nature of skills. Work experience in the last year at school can help young people, and secondment, experience of alternative employment, or job studies can help teachers; but such measures can have only limited success. Work demands and work conditions vary greatly and neither the direct experience of young people nor that of teachers will be adequate. Equally, it is arguable whether employers are able to give this information with sufficient accuracy. In Britain much is heard from employers about young people not being sufficiently literate and numerate for their purposes, and yet little information is available which will enable the nature and level of skills required to be pin-pointed. For what purposes, for example, do they need individuals who can read? Is it to enable them to follow instructions, to extract information, to make comparisons, to draw conclusions, to sort fact from opinion, etc.? Does the material to be read have a high technical content, etc.? Are calculations to be done using either a calculator or slide-rule? Is mental arithmetic required? Is it important to be familiar with both metric and imperial weights and measures, and to be able to convert one to the other? Do graphs or charts of one form or another have to be interpreted or drawn? Do dials have to be read and interpolations made? How likely is it that employees will have to present information numerically so that it can be handled by a computer or else interpret numerical print-out from a computer? As for employers' selection procedures, the extent to which these reflect skills actually needed in the job is open to question. Many employers rely heavily on the academic qualifications possessed by individuals. Some argue that they have little choice since this is the only real yardstick that the education system gives them to use. Certainly, in the present economic situation when there may be many applicants for any one job, using such qualifications as a cut-off point is one way of arriving at a manageable shortlist of candidates for interview. One is left wondering, however, whether many potentially good employees may be excluded by such a process. How relevant is it to use an essentially knowledge-based qualification to predict job-related skills such as operating precision equipment and instruments, determining the cause of machine breakdown, estimating the time needed to complete a piece of work, participating in group decision-making, showing others how to do things, persuading others in order to influence them towards some action or point of view, talking to customers or clients to put them at their ease, etc.? Some employers devise their own selection procedures and tests of basic skills such as literacy and numeracy, but it is open to question how closely the skills tested in selection relate to those on the job. It is all too rare to find selection procedures based on thorough analyses of jobs. The author has heard of cases recently when applicants have been required to carry out money calculations using pounds, shillings and pence!

The author's starting point, then, is the development of an analytical instrument designed to give a better understanding as to the nature, use and prevalence of skills in local labour markets. It is hypothesised that there exists a number of broad-based or common skills: that is, skills that are fundamental to the performance of many tasks carried out in a wide range of occupations. These are the skills that the author is attempting to identify and understand better. It is important to note that it is not being argued that by acquiring these skills a young person will be able to do jobs in all these occupations, but rather that he or she will have mastered the foundation upon which more specific job skills can be built. Yet the foundation is job-related because it is the result of an analysis of real jobs. Skills involving literacy and numeracy will be included, as will those involving aspects of verbal communication, reasoning, interpersonal behaviour and manipulative ability.

The author's approach to the design of such an analytical instrument is the development of a comprehensive inventory of these broad-based skills. For the purposes described, the inventory approach offers a number of advantages. First, it provides a relatively *rapid* and *cheap* means of collecting skill information. When the job holder or the supervisor are interviewed at the worksite, all they are required to do is to indicate by a simple 'yes' or 'no' whether a particular skill is used by the job holder. Since the inventory acts as a memory aid, they do not have to spend time recalling what is done in the job; nor do they have to spend time finding a form of words to express themselves—a particularly arduous task for less articulate workers. The technique becomes faster and cheaper still if the inventory is mailed to the job holder or supervisor for them to complete on their own. Obviously such a procedure would not be introduced unless checks had been made as to the accuracy of the replies given under these circumstances. In addition, the inventory would have to be well tested to ensure that the job holder or the supervisor readily understood the description of each skill, and that no skill description was ambiguous. A further advantage of an inventory is that it readily allows for *comparisons* to be made between jobs since it limits and controls the language used for description. Human language contains some redundancy and many subtleties. On the one hand, it is often possible to have a choice of words by which to convey a particular meaning, and yet, on the other hand, an individual word frequently has several meanings. For someone receiving and synthesising all the information at some central point, this makes it very difficult to compare one job with another. Different words may have been used to describe the same skill and the same words may have been used to describe skills which are subtly different. An inventory provides a standardised way of describing skills, and thus enables comparisons to be made more easily between different jobs. The final advantage of an inventory is that because it provides a relatively cheap, fast and effortless procedure for collecting skill information about jobs and for making comparisons, it becomes feasible to *up-date* this information at regular intervals. This up-dating process is important, since, particularly for industries which are in a fast technological stream, the nature of the skills needed changes quickly over time. Some young people currently at the beginning of their training are likely to be taught skills which will be obsolescent when their training is complete.[4]

In the development of an inventory of broad-based skills considerable help is being given by the Canadian Department of Manpower and Immigration. As in Britain, the Canadians are faced with high youth unemployment and one of the initiatives taken in the early seventies was the development of an analytical instrument along the lines which interest the author.[5] During 1977, a week was spent with the principal researcher discussing his work and seeing examples of its application in the Canadian provinces. A further four weeks was spent in lengthy discussions with other North American researchers who are leaders in the development of skill inventories of one kind or another.[6] A great deal of their expertise is being made use of in the development of a skills inventory in this country.

Mention has been made of analysing skills within a locality. Local labour markets have been chosen as the focal points for the analysis because this is where most young people expect to find employment. A Government Social Survey[7] shows that almost half of the people in the sample had lived at their present address for twenty years or more. Of the people who moved, the great majority remained in the same town. It is considered important that the analytical procedure be designed so as to be readily understood and used in a locality by those most concerned with establishing links between the education system and the labour market, i.e. those directly involved with the education, training and employment of young people. (It is all too easy to design a system so that it then needs an expert to handle it.) Earlier it was mentioned that the impact of unemployment is most severe on those young people who have few or no marketable skills or qualifications. In attempting to improve the link between the education system and the labour market, therefore, full account is being taken of that part of the labour market which contains jobs for which less academic 16 year olds can reasonably be expected to compete.

So far some three hundred descriptors have been developed to cover aspects of mathematical, communication, reasoning, interpersonal and manipulative skills. Only a proportion of these descriptors will be applicable to any particular job. In the work of a receptionist, for example, it might be expected that a lot of the skill descriptors in the interpersonal area might be relevant, but only comparatively few of the manipulative ones. The reverse might be true for the job of panel beater.

At present these broad-based skill descriptors are being pilot-tested in a local labour market by using them to profile a small sample of jobs. Since the part of the labour market which is of most interest to the author is that containing work for which less academic young people could reasonably be expected to compete, the sample contains jobs such as clerks, receptionists, secretaries, warehouse persons, picture framers, panel beaters, sales assistants, waiters and waitresses etc. An attempt has been made to include a range of jobs which will give an interesting spread of different types of skills, and for which vacancies are likely to occur. Some jobs have been included on the basis that in terms of their difficulty level they might be near the upper limit for the group of young people of primary interest. Both large and small organisations have been included in the sample. So far the response from employers has been very encouraging: most have been interested in the project and very prepared to help. Some have offered a wider range of jobs for study than that asked for, and others have offered access to the company again in the future.

At present both the job holder and the immediate supervisor are being interviewed with the skills inventory in order to find out how closely they agree as to the broad-based skills needed for the job. It is the skills used in the work which are of interest rather than all those possessed by the job holder. An individual may, for example, have acquired a wide range of manipulative skills and yet use very few of them in the current job.

For each descriptor, job holder and supervisor are being asked first to judge whether the broad-based skill is used in the job. If it is, then they are asked whether it is needed on job entry or whether it is taught to the individual (either on or off the job) once he has started work. Obviously, the dividing line between skills taught on the job and those needed on entry is unlikely to remain fixed over time. When there is a shortage of labour (unlike the situation for many jobs today) employers are more likely to be prepared to provide additional coaching so that individuals can cope with the job. From the very small sample of jobs examined so far, it seems that in addition there is a lot of variation between employers as to the importance they attach to skill level on entry. Some employers seem to be very demanding, whereas others appear to attach more importance to the personal qualities of the applicant and the interest shown in the job, etc.

Experiments are planned to test the usefulness of collecting additional information about the broad-based skills needed for jobs. In one experiment job holders and supervisors will be asked to rate each skill in terms of its importance for overall performance in the job. An individual may, for example, be very good at explaining and demonstrating how he does his work. If, however, he is only required to make use of the skills involved once a year when the organisation has an open day, then they may be rated as relatively unimportant in terms of their effect on overall performance in the job. On the other hand, skills such as those involved in the shutdown of a plant in a chemical industry may be rated as very important because, although used very infrequently, they may be crucial in an emergency situation, such as a chemical reaction going out of control. It is also planned to experiment with collecting information about the sorts of situations in which the broad-based skills are used. An air hostess, for example, is likely to talk to passengers in order to put them at their ease. A hotel receptionist may use the same skill when dealing with guests as might a personal assistant when talking to clients. It is thought that detailed examples as to the sorts of situations in which the skills are used may be useful for the design of curricula.

There is still a lot of experimentation to be done before the final list of broad-based skills is arrived at, together with the exact wording to be used to describe each skill. It still remains to be decided whether both the job holder and the immediate supervisor are to be interviewed, or only one of these individuals, and whether they are to be asked for information in addition to which skills are needed for the job (such as the skills needed on job entry). It is planned, however, that by the end of 1978 data collection should have begun in one local labour market. Arrangements are being made to work with the relevant local education authority over the next two years. It is hoped that teachers from the authority will be seconded to contribute their expertise to the development of the analytical instrument as well as helping with the interviewing in companies and the development of skill profiles for jobs. The skills information is intended for use by the local education authority in some of its colleges of further education, where pilot courses are being developed for unemployed school leavers. Much of the data collected, however, will it is believed, be of interest to those involved with secondary education.

School and work: an exchange of information

It may be that there is a very real possibility of an important bonus resulting from the development and use of such an analytical tool. A new recognition of the importance of vocational preparation at secondary as well as initial training level may bring the education system, the labour market services, employers and unions, etc., together for discussions. Employers, for example, complain about the lack of basic skills possessed by young people; young people complain that school has helped them little in mastering the uncertainties and complexities of adult life, including life at work; teachers complain that employers offer young people jobs which positively encourage a mindless approach. Improved information about the skills needed for jobs in a locality may be the means by which the contestants can get together for constructive discussions and joint action.

As to teachers complaining that some jobs positively require a mindless approach, the author is left wondering whether to some small extent the education system may have contributed to this. One important reason for employers designing jobs which are fragmented, proceduralised, routine, highly prescribed, etc. is that they then require a smaller amount of initial training. Perhaps if the education system took more account of the needs of the world of work, employers would feel that there was less need to organise work in this way. There is some evidence to suggest that for a given technology, it is often possible to organise work in a number of different ways, thus allowing workers to a greater or lesser extent to deploy skills and responsibility.[8] There may be some evidence to suggest that the vocational preparation of young people, before and once they are on the labour market, actively influences the way in which employers organise their work.[9] Taking account of the world of work does not mean that the education system has to slavishly respond to it. By focusing on best practices, the education system may be able to raise the standards of industry with respect to work organisation.

Once teachers and employers, etc. start examining the data collected by means of the analytical instrument, its limitations will inevitably come to light. When selecting individuals, employers are interested in personal qualities as well as skills, so account will need to be taken of this separately. There is evidence from recent surveys carried out by the Manpower Services Commission,[10] that employers are becoming increasingly concerned about the need for flexible individuals who can respond quickly to changing patterns of skill need and deployment. Employers say, for example, that if technological change is to be accepted by unions, every attempt must be made to continue to employ individuals, albeit they may be required to develop and use different skills. Under these circumstances, qualities such as 'learning how to learn' are likely to become increasingly important. Again, it is discussions between teachers, employers, unions, labour market services, etc. which will reveal such needs, rather than the use of the analytical instrument itself.

Examination of the data collected, together with discussions between teachers and employers, etc., is likely to have implications for the design of curricula, teaching methods, assessment, and certification. It is for colleagues better qualified than the author to discuss these implications. One or two comments will, however, be made. Firstly, everything that has been said in this chapter has emphasised the importance of 'being competent in' rather than 'knowing about'. This does not mean that knowledge is unimportant. Indeed, as a storehouse of all acquired human experiences and understanding, values and judgements, it is a paramount requirement. It is being argued, however, that knowledge should be primarily a guide to action – it is the outcomes of the action which should be used to test and validate the actions; these in turn will validate and modify the knowledge-base from which further action could be mounted.[11] This seriously brings into question the adequacy of the present system of certification. Secondly, for numbers of young people it appears that the most successful and motivating forms of learning do not take place exclusively in an educational institution. Some young people are seen to 'blossom' under schemes such as work experience. This suggests the importance of involving employers as well as other members of the community to a greater extent.

There are other reasons for involving employers. Firstly, they will be one of the main customers for any new forms of certification. Having them involved from the beginning makes it more likely that they will accept the changes. Secondly, whatever form of certification is used, it is likely that employers will be tempted to interpret it in such a way that the 'best' individual is selected. It is important, therefore, that they should be encouraged to examine their jobs carefully and realistically, and to assess the implications of the findings in terms of the sort of individual they ought to be looking for. A closer examination of jobs may even result in some exployers changing them in such a way that individuals are able to deploy more skills and responsibility.

References

1   *Young People and Work* Manpower Services Commission, London, 1977
2   Colledge, M., Llewellyn, G. and Ward, V. *Young People and Work* HMSO, 1978
3   *Census 1971 Great Britain: Economic Activity, Part III (10% sample)* HMSO, 1975
4   *Training for Skills: A Programme for Action*, Manpower Services Commission, 1977, pp. 24, 25
5   Smith, Arthur De W. *Generic Skills: Research and Development Training* Research and Development Station, Prince Albert, Saskatchewan, Canada, 1975
6   Freshwater, M. R. and Townsend, C. *Analytical Techniques for Skill Comparison: A Report Describing Some North American Approaches,* Vols 1 and 2, Psychological Services, Manpower Services Commission, 1978
7   Harris, A. I., and Clausen, P. *Government Social Survey: Labour Mobility in Great Britain 1953–63* HMSO, 1967
8   Hayes, F. C., *Groundwork for a Flexible Future* in Personnel Management March 1978
9   Hayes, F. C. *op. cit.*
10 *Training for Skills: A Programme for Action* Manpower Services Commission, 1977
11 Chambers, J. *Alternative Curricular Pathways for the Education and Training of 14–19 year old Youngsters? – A Critique of Present Provision: Institutional or Individual Needs?* The Association of Colleges for Further and Higher Education, from the Honorary Secretary, ACFHE, Sheffield City Polytechnic, Pond Street, Sheffield S1 1WF

Part III
Outcomes of Education

13   Conclusions and proposals

ELIZABETH ADAMS AND TYRRELL BURGESS

The first two parts of this book have been concerned with the weaknesses of the present system of examinations for 16 year olds and, in more detail, with various attempts to record and report the outcomes of education at that stage. It is now time to build upon existing experience to show, at any rate in outline, that it is possible for all young people at the end of compulsory schooling to have something serious to show for their experience. We offer a suggestion for the kind of system that might be set up in a school, together with the arrangements that could be made for gaining public recognition and support. We also outline national arrangements through which each school's procedures could be given a national currency. We believe the proposals we make are practicable, and we discuss the kind of organisation which would accommodate such questions as the role of subject specialisms, the individual tutor, the organisation of the school day and staff/student ratios. At the heart of our proposals is a statement which every 16 year old will have on leaving school, showing his experience, competence, interests and purposes, which he can show to parents and employers alike.

It is important to realise that statements for 16 year olds cannot be compiled out of the blue in the last week or two at school. Like existing examinations, they will be the culmination of a programme of work which has covered the previous two years. It is our belief that these programmes will be immeasurably improved if young people themselves have the initiative in creating them, so that the content of the curriculum, the recording of its outcome and the measurement of achievement is planned, agreed and pursued jointly by young people and their teachers.

In such a programme there will be three main stages. It will begin at age 14 (at the end of the third year in England) when the initial plans will be drawn up; it will be reconsidered and revised a year later; and it will culminate at the age of 16, at the end of the fifth year, with a statement giving a positive account of the young person's attributes, competences and interests, together with proposals for the future.

The idea of a kind of planning period at the age of 14 is not in itself new. At present students of that age are asked in most secondary schools to consider the courses they are going to take in the next two years. They are asked to decide on their 'options'. Many schools take this process very seriously. They arrange tutorial and counselling sessions. They discuss future careers. They set aside time for questioning teachers. They arrange open evenings for parents, together with meetings to explain their 'options' scheme and the range of possibilities available.

The decisions which they are asking students and parents to make can have very serious consequences. To take one subject rather than another, or GCE rather than CSE, may not only affect the pupil's contentment and performance over the next two years but may also determine his life chances. Of course, schools vary in the extent to which they can accommodate pupils' wishes: some manage to satisfy almost all aspirations while meeting their own commitment to a 'balanced' course for all. In others the 'options' may seem more like a series of constraints on what combinations are possible. In some schools the wish of a student to pursue a particular course is respected (perhaps with appropriate warnings) even if the student does not show too much promise. In others, previous performance may in effect be decisive – with only those scoring well in a subject being allowed to take it for public examination.

But whatever the variation in present practice, there is clearly a moment in the life of almost every secondary school student when he or she has to consider his future programme and to take decisions which are very serious. It is with this moment that our own proposals begin.

We suggest that at the end of the summer term all 14 year olds should have a 'planning period' (to be determined by each school) in which they are asked to consider seriously how they will use the next two years of their time at school. As a start, they will be handed a copy of the blank statements which they and their teachers will complete together at the age of 16. The student will file this blank in a special folder in which over the next two years he is to collect evidence of the level and quality of his best work and of the nature of his chief interests. The object of the blank is to direct the student's mind from the start to the outcome of the process and remind him or her of the need to establish evidence of attainment.

The major part of the planning period, however, will be a chance for the students, perhaps for the first time, to consider themselves, their futures and what it is they need to do to make a success of both. In the first place they will be asked to make a summary of their skills, competences, attainments, interests and purposes as they see these at the end of the particular summer term in which the planning period takes place. This is in itself a difficult task. Self-knowledge comes with difficulty to most people. First attempts may be faltering and unimpressive, or expressed in merely conventional terms. On the other hand, within this process there will be time to think, to discuss with friends or teachers and to revise false starts. Students will be encouraged to say as fully as possible what it is that they do which is of importance to them. This may include achievement outside school, and it may include evidence of school achievement left unmeasured by school tests.

When students are used to thinking about what they are like now, and what it is they can best do, they will then be asked to consider, in the broadest outline, what it is they will want to do in two years' time at the end of compulsory schooling. Again, they will need a little help in this, in discussing jobs and futures. There is much which a 16 year old does which is unimaginable to a 14 year old. There will be a wide variety in the definition of career intentions: career choices are made at many different ages, not just at 14 or 16. At this stage, these intimations of the future may be vague and unconvincing. It will be part of the purpose of the programme for the next two years to introduce realism and rigour. Again, it will be important for students to be encouraged to state these hopes and possibilities in their own terms, without for the present being constrained by the set pattern of examinations, and accommodating what can be achieved outside as well as inside school.

At this point, the student will have two outlines: one of himself as he is at present and one (much more vague and incomplete) of what he would wish to be in two years' time. Most students will readily recognise that they have presented themselves with a problem: how to get from where they are now to where they want to be in the time available. They have presented their school with a problem too: how to help them to accomplish the task which they have set themselves. It is the solution to this problem that will constitute the student's educational programme over the next two years, and the creation of this programme is the task for the remainder of the planning period.

We believe that a process such as we have described will have four major advantages over the present arrangements. In the first place it will concentrate the students' minds on their education as a direct part of their own development and preparation for the future. It will greatly increase the 'relevance' which students commonly say is missing from school at present. Second, in giving students initiative, it offers the chance of changing what schools actually offer, by encouraging teachers to recognise those characteristics and achievements of students that are neglected by present arrangements. Third, and growing from this, it enables students and teachers to develop a new relationship of collaboration so that each can learn from the other. It will no longer be a matter of the teacher's presenting material for the student to take or leave, nor will it become a means for students to determine unilaterally what they want. It will be a process of mutual cooperation. Fourth, it forms the basis for a serious statement by school leavers about the nature of the outcome of their school experience.

When this initial draft programme has been completed, each student will take his own home for discussion with his parents. We believe it would make for a more fruitful discussion if parents were asked to sign the programme after adding any observations they wish to make. The student should then sign his programme and return it to his teacher by an appointed date. Each student's programme will be discussed by a small group of teachers. When it is agreed by them it will be signed by the teacher who is to have tutorial responsibility for the student during the next two years. Any difficulties which arise at this stage will be discussed with the student and amendments made accordingly. The original programme will be filed by the school and a copy filed by the student in his special folders.

During the first year of the programme each student will follow the course that has been agreed, according to the timetable which the school has evolved to accommodate it. Throughout the programme teachers will be responsible for the suitability of the nature and level of the work of each student and for its continuous recording and assessment – in accordance with each student's programme. Students too will be encouraged systematically to record their work and progress, and teachers will remind students periodically of the need to build up in their folders evidence of their best work and growing interests and will seek to see that the agreed programmes are being covered.

At the end of the first year there will be a second planning period, conducted on much the same lines as the first. Now, of course, the initial step of self-assessment will be on the basis of the records accumulated in the first year. It will be not only a statement of where students are now but an assessment of the extent to which they have completed their agreed programme. What is more, with experience students will want to reconsider their stated outcomes. Some may find their original ideas confirmed: others may want to make radical changes. This second planning period, therefore, may be easier than the first in that its processes will be more familiar and the basis for it less nebulous. It may be harder in that the students themselves will have a more realistic understanding of the problems which face them and will be dissatisfied with their earlier vagueness.

Again, these revised statements should be seen and signed by parents, after discussion with their children. They will be discussed by groups of teachers, and again one teacher with tutorial responsibility will sign them. It will be for the school to see that each student's programme for the next year can be practicably followed.

It is at the end of the second year of the programme and of compulsory education that the final preparation of statements will take place. By this time each student will have built up a folder containing evidence of skills and competences, of mastery of concepts and subject matter and of awareness and self-confidence in positive attributes and qualities. During the last year teachers will have helped students to check their folders and to remove superfluous or unworthy items. As an aid to putting and keeping the folder in order, it will have a contents sheet, made by the student, of all the items finally included. This sheet should be signed by the responsible teacher.

It is on the basis of the evidence in the folder that each student will prepare his or her final statement. This statement will be a positive account of the student's attributes, competences and interests, with proposals for the future. It will be an account of what can be said for the student at the end of the compulsory school stage. While public examinations exist at 16 plus, the statement might include reference to them. It is important, however, that there should be no subject or activity in which the only entry in the statement is an exam grade. Students should be asked to furnish other evidence of competences in the field and to say where the examination grade fits into this evidence.

On an appointed day the statement and its accompanying folder will become the property of the student whether or not he intends to return to school, and a copy of each statement will be retained at the school for at least three years. Before the appointed day, a student will be able to borrow his statement to take to an interview, or for some similar purpose.

Such a process as we have described builds upon and develops the practice of many schools in helping young people to decide about their future in school and afterwards. It will require all the experience which exists (examples of which are reported in Part II of this book) in recording the educational experience of students. Enough is known to suggest that our proposals are practicable. On the other hand it will not be enough for schools merely to repeat existing practice, however good, and substitute a new orthodoxy for existing examinations. The essence of our proposals is that students and their teachers think through their own problems and propose their own unique solutions. We see this individual initiative as offering an educative experience in itself. Clearly this implies a major increase in the teacher's professional responsibility. The move from externally established syllabuses to programmes created by teachers represented a similar growth of responsibility. Bringing in the initiative of students will make the teacher's sense of professionalism even more important.

The question that is raised by these suggestions is whether it is possible to organise schools in such a way that students can follow programmes which they themselves, with the help of their teachers, have planned. As we have emphasised earlier, we do not see it as our task to specify in detail the way in which we think schools should be run. It is central to what we are proposing that each individual school finds the form of organisation which grows most aptly out of its own purpose and performance. Nor do we believe that the organisation of a school can, or should be, changed overnight. Organisational change should be introduced gradually, so that it does not place additional burdens on staff or students. We have suggested that a new approach to the curriculum, which would arise from a better recording of the outcomes of education for each student at 16, could be introduced for students at the end of their third year at secondary school as an alternative to the decisions about 'options' which are at present common at that stage. In our view this would be a way of accommodating the inevitable transitional period. For clarity, however, we concentrate here on an outline organisation of a school after the change has been made.

Such an organisation would be very different from that which is typical of secondary schools today, and it is important to make the attempt to recognise present practice for what it is, to stand back from it and to think of alternatives untrammelled by it. In the traditional secondary school the students are divided into groups of twenty-five or thirty, and these groups often change as students are placed in streams, bands or sets. The school week is divided into thirty or more periods of perhaps forty minutes in length. During the week any student is likely to study ten or a dozen different subjects with perhaps an equal number of different teachers. In addition he may meet his form or class teacher, his house teacher, his year head and perhaps a guidance specialist or deputy head.

In the same way, a teacher may meet a considerable number of classes, sets or groups with varying numbers, involving him in rapid switching from one mode of conduct to another, and often even from one room to another. He may have tutorial responsibility for students whom he does not teach. In addition there may be lunchtime and after-school contacts.

It has been recognised in many schools that this number of contacts between students and teachers, together with the fragmentation of the academic week, disrupts concentration and makes demands for a multiplicity of human relationships that are difficult to sustain satisfactorily. It also has the effect of presenting knowledge to students as distinct 'subjects' unrelated either to each other or to life outside school.

Already a number of schools are seeking to mitigate the unhappy effects of this by such devices as 'double periods' or by devoting whole mornings or afternoons to particular 'subjects'. Very often elaborate 'tutorial' arrangements are made to ensure the particular responsibility of teachers for the whole work of individual students.

Our suggestions build upon such developments as these. They rest on the belief that the basis of every student's work should be a personal relationship with a particular teacher which continues through his stay in the school. The overall staffing levels of secondary schools are in our view sufficient to make this relationship a fruitful one if all the teaching resources are used. In 1976 the overall student–teacher ratio in secondary schools in England and Wales was 17 to 1. Our proposals would require that all teachers in a school accepted a tutorial responsibility. Excluding the head, and allowing for absences, they would work with a ratio of 20 to 1. If each teacher is to see each of the twenty students for whom he is responsible for half an hour a week, it would require a total of ten hours or, say, four afternoons. It is clearly possible to arrange the school timetable not in individual periods of forty minutes each but in 'blocks' of tutorial time. During this time, for a total of ten hours a week, students would be in their permanent home bases with their tutors. Each student would use the time in two main ways: in preparing a report for his tutor and in working on his specialist studies which we describe later. The tutorial group itself might contain, as 'house' systems do at present, students of various ages. The tutorial group would place upon students the obligation to engage in supervised individual learning, preparation, completion of assignments and other academic problems for perhaps two-fifths of their time in school.

At the same time the tutor would have the obligation to discuss with each of his students the latter's programme and performance, the progress he had made towards the eventual completion of a statement and any difficulties, pastoral or academic, that might arise. Every teacher in the school would have, as a basic part of his work, and whatever his other duties, such a tutorial relationship with perhaps twenty students. This central and substantial responsibility would be to ensure not only that the student engaged in his own work during the time appointed but that this work was directed towards goals that had already been agreed.

It is important not to underestimate the gains in this for the individual teacher. Not only does it make possible a serious and productive relationship with individual students: it would also give every teacher, of whatever specialism, an irreplaceable insight into the working of the rest of the school. It would produce, naturally, innumerable occasions for the teacher to collaborate with colleagues and to develop interests of his own not tapped by the existing rigid subject barriers. It would make the tutorial relationship one of collaborative learning. Even a teacher who was weak in, say, mathematics, would be able to assist one of his students by the simple process of requiring the purpose and content of the work to be explained. This new relationship would undoubtedly demand different skills from teachers, but they are skills which the relationship would itself be the most powerful aid and spur to develop.

The rest of the week would be 'blocked' for the specialist studies which each student had agreed to undertake in the course of preparing his programme. The precise organisation of this must be determined after the students' programmes have been agreed. One solution would be for groups of teachers to combine to offer to meet the needs of groups of students in picked fields of inquiry such as science, engineering, aesthetics, economic and social studies, English or English and philosophy, foreign languages and cultures. These groups are not exhaustive or exclusive. For some students physical education might be grouped with aesthetics. For others science and engineering might be combined. For some students mathematics might be a field of inquiry on its own, for others it might be as a service to students in the natural or social sciences. There is a place in all fields for clear thought and expression which is traditionally offered by teachers of English.

The important organisational need is to simplify the timetable into 'blocks', so that students and teachers know broadly their tasks for particular periods of time, but leaving each free to combine in ways that seem best in the light of the students' programmes. Some schools may find they wish to continue to organise these studies in 'years'. Others may mix students of different ages according to the stage of their understanding of particular fields. One school may offer to a year group a different broadly blocked 'field' on each morning of the week. Another might make it possible for students to concentrate on a field for half a term at a time.

What is important is not a particular form of organisation – though it *is* important to break the present distracting rigidities – but the realisation that new patterns are possible and potentially creative. The principle of school organisation outlined here rests upon the twin foundations of serious individual tuition and the growth of individual learning in broad academic fields. Different schools will evolve different patterns. Both teachers and students would work together long enough to know each other and to explore together the specialist fields of interest. Each would learn from the other: students from students, students from teachers and teachers from students.

The proposals which we make here would make a radical difference to the schools, but the changes would come from the actions of students and teachers. In this they would be quite different from other proposed changes, of curriculum or examinations, which are designed outside the school and are then imposed with more or less acceptance from those affected. Our proposals, on the other hand, are not a generalised solution, but a framework in which an infinite variety of solutions can be sought by students and teachers. It is a means by which schools can change without compulsion, giving teachers and students a greater ability to meet each other's needs and the needs of society.

For example, we have said that the planning period we propose is a development of the process of deciding on 'options' which already takes place. The fact that it is such a development makes its introduction possible with the minimum of stress and upheaval. But the process of planning is different from the process of choosing, as teachers and students would quickly discover. The decision to take one O level course rather than another will have a different quality when it is set in a total programme which is seen both as a solution to present problems and a preparation for what is to come. A planning period which begins with the initiative of students rather than with predetermined curricula radically alters the relationship between students and teachers, as John Stephenson has earlier made clear. Similarly, the tutorial relationship which already exists in many schools would gain in reality and purpose from monitoring and revising a planning agreement to which both sides were committed.

Our proposals deliberately do not assume any particular learning method, because we believe the planning process is adaptable to existing practice in schools. But we are quite sure that the process would greatly influence this practice, and schools would find themselves evolving new methods of organisation and new modes of learning as they sought to accommodate the expressed needs of students. In time we should expect to find more individual programmes and more individual instruction than is common in fourth and fifth forms at present.

We recognise that our proposals have profound implications for teachers – all of them, in our view, beneficial. The outcomes of education for students depend on the competences of teachers. At present these competences are mainly related to examinations because examinations have dominated the teachers' own education, training and professional experience. Developing student programmes and producing statements of individual outcomes calls for other competences, not hitherto much recognised in the school system. Whatever their sex, age or background, few teachers will ever have been asked to help to make a programme for their own education, nor asked to help boys and girls to do so. Entry to the profession and promotion within it are normally achieved without serious reference to the outcome of teachers' work as shown by their students.

It is not that teachers themselves all fail to recognise that the art of teaching lies in the interaction between teacher and student. The trouble is to identify 'good' teaching. In practice, heads and inspectors try to help 'good' teachers to gain promotion, but in the absence of statements describing the outcomes for individual students at 16, their recommendations are unnecessarily subjective, even idiosyncratic. In any case, the best place for good teachers is the classroom, not the office. In Britain so far neither educational research nor the Great Debate has thrown up much in the way of leads towards the recognition of good teaching. So far, the gap between the avowed aims of education and the identifiable outcomes for individual 16 year olds remains unbridged.

The question of judging competence is important for students and teachers alike. In Britain the Manpower Services Commission is working to identify life skills related to employment. Given the attention it deserves, such work sheds light on the disservice done to the nation's economy by inadequate description of the outcomes of education. At the Institute of Competence Assessment factors differentiating superiority in human service have been validated in the medical profession, in US Navy training and in the Massachusetts Civil Service. Work is advancing on the testing of different areas of competence such as problem solving, moral reasoning, concern for building good working associations, non-verbal sensitivity, concern for doing one's duty, and general characteristics of the individual regarding the way he thinks about the world and himself, the way he reacts to new information and the way he behaves. Paul Pottinger has described some of these researches in an article 'Techniques and Criteria for Designing and Selecting Instruments for Assessing Teachers'. His suggestions are for new ways to judge a teacher's competence. To undertake such a series of tests as he outlines would, in itself, provide students and teachers with a learning experience regarding the competences needed by teachers. It might help to smooth the introduction into schools of the system of programmes and 16 plus statements outlined in this book.

Some such procedure could also help to ensure understanding of the new requirements regarding programmes and statements as compared with the present familiar system of examinations. The successful introduction of the system outlined in this book could ameliorate the crisis of accountability in education currently destroying the confidence alike of teachers, students, parents and the public at large.

The problem about developing relevant competences in teachers will diminish over the years as the new demands on their professional expertise become familiar. Moreover, as schools come to provide the conditions under which students and teachers work together more responsibly, increasing numbers of young people will display the problem-solving competences in which they were trained at school. These habits and disciplines fit the pattern of a general recurrent education widely anticipated in Europe by OECD and others. In fact, they can only help people no matter what life holds in store for them.

There is one function of the education system for which our proposals have profound implications, and that is social and vocational selection. We believe this function has had too little explicit discussion. It is almost wholly omitted from the educational theory which is offered to teachers in training. It is assumed without question by, for instance, employers who demand reliable certification at various levels. Discussions between student, parents and teachers are often muddled because the student imagines them to be about a unique person (himself), whereas the teacher is thinking of levels, categories and classification. The parent, knowing both the student and something of the demands of the world outside school, uneasily tries to accommodate both.

There are two major attitudes to the use of the educational system for selective processes among those who have thought about it deeply. The first recognises that the measures used are unsatisfactory in themselves and irrelevant to any need outside schools. In this view what is needed is a radical revision of the instruments of assessment. On the other hand there are those who believe that education cannot even in principle be used as a selector without destroying itself. Selection, they argue, is not only incompatible with education but is anti-educational. On this view school assessment should not be used at all in selecting students for employment or some further stage of education. As Elsa Davies suggested earlier, the development of education in primary schools has depended upon the ending of its use as a selector for different kinds of secondary schools.

Our proposals offer an alternative to this dilemma. We believe that a statement of the outcomes of education for an individual, as a culmination of a programme which the individual has himself planned and carried through, not only gives promise of a valid educational experience, but forms a basis upon which young people themselves, their parents, future employers or other educational establishments can make rational decisions. Don Stansbury has shown that it is not only possible for people outside schools to handle unstandardised information in making judgements about people but that this kind of information is in fact more useful. It is the categories and standards, the passes and grades, which are empty and misleading. The information they convey and their predictive value are almost nil.

We believe that it is possible for schools to make progress along these lines, whatever happens to examinations at 16 plus. The contributions in Part II make it clear how far individual teachers and schools can go. We suggest that our proposals would be preferable to any existing or proposed system of examining at 16 plus, and we hope that many more schools will make their own innovations. Colin Fletcher's article makes it clear, however, that schools are highly vulnerable if their staffs have to carry too heavy a weight of innovation on their own, particularly if they come under political attack. There must be some way in which initiative can be supported. It is important to make it clear that schools need support, not mere defence. Support must include acceptable ways in which they can be accountable and make proposals for improvement. Unfortunately the present tendency of insisting on the publication of league tables of examination performance can lead only to none-too-scrupulous harassment. What the public needs, instead, is the assurance that each school is serving its own students as well as possible in its own unique circumstances.

For this purpose, we now propose a way in which the school can gain the help of all those concerned with it, from its own governing body and local education authority to the national curriculum agencies, like the Schools Council, to secure recognition for its own initiatives.

For this, both teachers and students need external validation to give them confidence in what they are doing and to secure its acceptance by the world outside. Since the procedures will differ from one school to another the public at large, the local authority and ultimately the Secretary of State need to feel that what each school is doing is valid in its own circumstances.

We therefore propose that each school should establish an external validating board to review the process by which the students plan their programmes. Its chairman might aptly be the chairman of the governing body (to which the local authority, under present arrangements, has delegated the general direction of the conduct and curriculum of the school). Its members might include such people as a major local employer, the chairman of the chamber of commerce or trades council, a teacher from another school or a lecturer from a local college, a local authority adviser or some other person with professional competence in education. They should all be people of known competence and reputation. The clerk to the validating board should be the head teacher or the teacher with overall responsibility for the two-year programme.

The major purpose of the board is to see that the process which the school has established is consistent and is working as intended. (It is *not* to lay down what that process should be: that is a professional matter.) It will judge how far the agreements made by students and teachers can reasonably be said to give promise that their purpose will be fulfilled and can culminate in the production of a final statement. The board can do this only by discussing individual programmes with individual students and their teachers. It should therefore have access to all the programmes created during the planning period, and it should see the students and teachers concerned in a random sample of these. Its judgements, however, will be gathered together and expressed in general terms. It might say, for example, that on the basis of the programmes it had seen, the board was confident that the school's procedures were apt for their purpose and that on the whole programmes were well designed to achieve the students' purposes: on the other hand, the school should consider whether or not the time available for planning was too short for pupils to do themselves justice.

For most of its general discussions (as opposed to individual meetings of board members with students and teachers) the validating board would meet with those teachers with major responsibility for the two-year programmes. The board might also set aside a time for a private discussion about the things it had seen and on the shape of its final report. This report should be circulated to all the teachers in the school and to the governing body. A copy should be lodged with the local education authority.

The idea of external validation of programmes is probably new to most teachers, but most will readily see that some such arrangements become necessary when individual teachers and students themselves carry greater responsibility. This kind of external moderation is very much more familiar in assessment and examination. In higher education, for example, courses in universities and colleges all have external examiners. GCE and CSE boards have arrangements for mutual moderation of their examinations. If students are to offer evidence of their experience and achievement other than that provided by external examinations, accrediting procedures are necessary to prevent injustice to students, to build up a body of knowledge about the outcomes of compulsory education and to monitor these outcomes in different schools. Both teachers and students need to know how far their standards and judgements are comparable with those being made elsewhere. The public at large needs the assurance that there is no carelessness or corruption in particular institutions.

A system of statements for 16 year olds requires that each school has an internal accrediting board to offer the kind of reassurance which is offered by the assessment boards of institutions of post-school education. There is already plenty of experience in further education of establishing such boards. Broadly speaking, they consist of the staff centrally responsible for the programme, together with colleagues with other responsibilities, to secure the support of the whole institution for what the assessment board is doing. In addition there should be a number of external assessors drawn from other schools and colleges, the inspectorate and any other groups of people who might be apt for particular programmes.

It will be the duty of the accrediting board to consider the completed statements of 16 year olds, to look in detail at sample statements and if necessary to meet particular 16 year olds and their teachers. Their object would be to confirm the content of the statements as an acceptable reflection of the capacities and attributes of the students. It would offer advice upon the various forms of assessment that students and their teachers had evolved.

It is important that the validating and accrediting boards should be separate. The jobs they have to do are different. The first validates planned programmes. The second gives accreditation to statements about outcomes. On the other hand it might well be helpful for each board to have an observer at the meetings of the other. Again, reports of the accrediting board would be distributed to teachers and governors and a copy lodged with the local education authority.

So far we have proposed a system in which the planning of students and their teachers, together with the final statements that emerge from compulsory schooling, are made acceptable to young people and their parents and in the general locality of the school. To have secured that much is very important, but it is not enough. We now have to make proposals through which the statements of 16 year olds can be seen to have a national currency. It is important that a young person can take a statement to an employer or to an educational institution in any part of the country without the risk of its being rejected as unknown or distrusted. Fortunately there are many precedents for achieving this. The national certificate scheme in further education gave national currency to locally created courses through joint boards of the Department of Education and Science and the professional institutions. The Council for National Academic Awards validates courses created by individual institutions. Mode III of the CSE is a way of gaining general currency for a course created in a particular school. It is also helpful to remember that the standard of degrees in universities is maintained, not by an assurance that all courses, even in a particular subject, are the same, but through public confidence in the *process* of creating and running degree courses. What is needed, therefore, is a way of creating public confidence in the process by which statements are produced in individual schools. The body which has overall national responsibility for this is presumably the Schools Council for the Curriculum and Examinations. It is of course physically impossible for the Schools Council to have an individual relationship with every secondary school in England. The body which has overall responsibility for the curriculum locally (for 'secular instruction' in the words of the Education Act 1944) is the local education authority – except insofar as it delegates this responsibility to governing bodies. On the other hand, the local authorities also need some way of knowing whether their own schools are comparable with those elsewhere. It seems therefore that a national system for validating statements for 16 year olds should be administered through bodies established by groups of local authorities and reporting to the Schools Council. Each of these joint councils should have an independent chairman and its own staff with assessors from the local inspectorate and HMI. It should be responsible for reviewing the procedures established by schools and for the standards of statements (not, of course, for the standard of work reflected, which is a matter for assessment but for the standard of the reporting). Each council should report annually to a convocation consisting of the chairmen of the accrediting board of each school. The council itself should be representative of all the major interests: local authorities, teachers, parents, industry and commerce, other educational institutions and bodies.

What we have tried to do in this book is to show that the need for reform in recording the outcomes of education is urgent, to report the hopeful experience on which such reform can be based and to outline the kind of structure which would make it possible. We believe that the most promising course is to establish a system, nationally validated, offering to everyone at the end of compulsory schooling a statement about his educational experience. Elements of the system already exist. What is important now is for a number of schools to develop statements along the lines we suggest, so as to show what can be achieved in practice. At the same time they can create their own means of validation and accreditation that would secure support for their innovation. We need bold proposals, well tested. For this purpose, the contributors to this book are helping to establish a numbers of pilot schemes in particular schools or areas through which the kind of system we have described can be set up, at any rate at local level. They are establishing a network through which such pilot schemes might be monitored. Schools interested in participating are asked to get in touch with Tyrrell Burgess, 34 Sandilands, Croydon, CRO 5DB, or with Elizabeth Adams, 29 Woodside House, London, SW19 7QN.

Selected references on recording the outcomes of education

Alexander, W. and Farrell, J. P., *Student Participation in Decision Making*, OISE, 252 Bloor Street, Toronto, 1975

Auld, Report: *William Tyndale Jnr and Infants Schools Public Enquiry*, ILEA, *1976* (See Paragraph 848)

Beloe Report: *Secondary School Examinations other than GCE*, HMSO 1960 (See paragraph 130; also see Appendixes for excerpts relating to school records quoted from several earlier reports)

Bloom, B. S. *et al.*, *Handbook on Formative and Summative Evaluation of Student Learning*, McGraw Hill, New York, 1971

Bloomfield, B., Dobby, J., and Kendall, L., *Ability and Examinations at 16+*, Schools Council Research Studies, Macmillan Education, 1979

Brimer, A., Madans, G. F., *et al.*, *Sources of Difference in School Achievement*, NFER Publishing, 1978

Broadfoot, Patricia, *Assessment, Schools and Society*, Methuen, 1979

Burgess, T., *Education After School*, Gollancz and Penguin, 1977

Choppin, B. *Item Banking and the Monitoring of Achievement*, NFER Research in Progress series 1, 1978

Cohen, L. and Deal, R. N., *Assessment by Teachers in Examinations at 16+*, Schools Council Examinations Bulletin 37, Evans/Methuen Educational, 1977

Curriculum 11–16, DES, HMSO 1976

Deale, R. N., *Assessment and Testing in the Secondary School*, Schools Council Examinations Bulletin 32, Evans/Methuen, 1975

Dobby, H. and Duckworth, D., *Objective Assessment by means of Item Banking*, Evans/Methuen Educational, 1979

Dockrell, W. B. & Black, H. D., *Assessment in the Affective Domain: What Can Be Done About It?* Scottish Council for Research in Education, 1978

Enquiry 1: Young School Leavers, Report of an enquiry carried out for the Schools Council by the Government Social Survey, HMSO, 1968

Flanagan, J. C., et al., *Personal and Social Performance Record: Teachers Guide and Materials*, American Institutes for Research, Palo Alto, Calif. and Science Research Association, (recently re-published) 1958

Fletcher, C., and Thompson, N. T. (ed.), *Issues in Community Education*, Falmer Press, 1979

Foster, J., *Recording Individual Progress*, Macmillan Education, 1971

Furth, D., *Selection and Certification in Education and Employment* OECD, Paris, 1977

Harlen, W. (ed.), *Evaluation and the Teacher's Role*, Schools Council Research Study, Macmillan Education, 1979

Hoste, R. and Bloomfield, B., *Continuous Assessment in the CSE: Opinion and Practice*, Schools Council Examinations Bulletin 31, Evans/Methuen Educational, 1975

Ingenkamp, K., *Educational Assessment*, Council of Europe, NFER, 1977

Klemp, G. O., *Three Factors of Success in the world of work: Implications for Curriculum in Higher Education*, McBer, Boston, 1977

Magnusson, O., *Education and Employment: the problems of early school leavers*, Institut d'Education, Paris, 1978

Miller, C. M. L. and Barlett, M., *Up to the Mark: a Study of the Examination Game*, Society for Research into Higher Education, 1974

Montgomery, R., *Examinations: an Account of their Evolution as Administrative Devices in England*, Routledge and Kegan Paul, 1965

Montgomery, R., *A New Examination of Examinations*, Routledge & Kegan Paul, 1978

Neave, G., *How They Fared: the impact of the comprehensive school upon the University*, Routledge and Kegan Paul, 1975

Neave, G., *Patterns of Equality: influence of New Structures in European Higher Education*, NFER, 1976

Neave, G. and MacPherson, A., *The Scottish Sixth: the changing relationship between school and university in Scotland*, NFER, 1976

Neave, G. (ed.), *Research Perspectives on the Transition from School to Work*, Swets and Zeitlinger, Amsterdam, 1977

Nuttall, D. S., and Willmott, A. S., *British Examinations: Techniques of Analysis*, NFER, 1972

Rance, P., *Record Keeping in the Progressive Primary School*, Ward Lock Educational, 1970

Rauta, I. and Hunt, A., *Fifth Form Girls: their Hopes for the Future*, Office of Population Censuses and Surveys, Social Survey Division, HMSO, 1975

Pupils' Progress Records, Report of a Working Party appointed by the Secretary of State for Scotland, HMSO, 1969

Raven, J., *Education, Values and Society: the Objectives of Education and the Nature and Development of Competence*, London, H. K. Lewis, London, and The Psychological Corporation, New York, 1977

Schools Council Working Paper 53, *The Whole Curriculum 13–16*, Evans/Methuen Educational, 1975 (see final summary)

Scottish Council for Research in Education, *Pupils in Profile: Making the Most of Teachers' Knowledge of Pupils*, Hodder and Stoughton, 1977 (Details from SCRE, 16 Moray Place, Edinburgh. Materials on order from Safeguard Business Systems, Loomer Road, Chesterton, Newcastle, Staffs.)

Stansbury, D., *Record of Personal Experience, Qualities and Qualifications, Tutor's Handbook*, RPE Publications, 25 Church Street, South Brent, Devon

Sumner, R., *Monitoring National Standards of Attainment in Schools*, NFER, 1977

Taylor Report: *A New Partnership for our Schools*, HMSO, 1977

Torshen, K. P., *The Mastery Approach to Competency-Based Education*, Academic Press, 1977

Vincent, D., and Cresswell, M., *Reading Tests in the Classroom*, NFER, 1976

Waddell Report: *School Examinations*, Parts I and II Cmnd. 7281, HMSO, 1978

Walker, David, A., *The IEA Six Subject Survey: an Empirical Study of Education In Twenty-one Countries*, John Wiley, Halsted Press, 1976

Willmott, A. S. and Nuttall, D. L., *The Reliability of Examinations at 16 plus*, Schools Council Research Studies, Macmillan Education, 1975

Willmott, A. S., and Fowles, D. E., *The Objective Interpretation of Test Performance – the Rasch Model Applied*, NFER, Slough, 1974

Willmott, A. S., and Nuttall, D. L., *The Reliability of Examinations at 16+*, Schools Council Research Studies, Macmillan Education, 1975

Wright, Nigel, *Progress in Education*, Croom Helm, 1977

Articles

Accreditation of Adolescents, from Education Offices, Liverpool

Adams, E. and Dean, J., 'School Records' in *Journal of NAIEA* No. 4, Summer 1975, from Harold Heaps, 8 Oakfield Avenue, Birstall, Leics

Armytage, W. H. G., 'The Docimological Dilemma: Quality Control or Quantity Surveying?', the Galton Lecture, 1974 in Cox *et al.*, (ed.), *Equalities and Inequalities in Education*, Academic Press, 1975

Assessing the Performance of Pupils, DES Report on Education Number 93, free with other APU leaflets from Room 2/1 Elizabeth House, York Road, London, S. E. 1

Benjamin, I., *As it was: Sutton Centre School 1976/77*, from Research Office Sutton Centre, High Pavement, Sutton-in-Ashfield, Notts.

Broadfoot, P. M., 'Trends in Assessment: A Scottish Contribution to the Debate', in *Trends in Education*, 1971/2, HMSO

Broadfoot, P. M., 'Communication in the Classroom: the role of assessment in motivation', in *Educational Review*, Spring 1979

Deale, R., 'The Assessment Jungle', in *Dialogue* 23, Autumn 1976, Schools Council Publishing

Dunnette, M. D., 'Assessing Aptitudes, Abilities and Skills' in Dunnette, M. D. (ed.), *A Handbook of Organizational Psychology*, 1976

Education in Schools: a Consultative Document, Green Paper, Cmnd. 6869, HMSO

Examples of Mode III with Maximum Casework Assessment, Hreod Burna School, Swindon

Flanagan, J. C., and Burns, R. K. 'The Employee Performance Record: a new appraisal and development tool', in *Harvard Business Review* year and vol. unknown, 95–102.

Forrest, G. M. (ed.), *A Scheme of Examining in Biology (Ordinary) Involving the Assessment of Course Work*, JMB, Manchester, 1977

Goldstein, H. and Blinkhorn, S., 'Monitoring Educational Standards – an inappropriate model', in *Bulletin* of the British Psychological Society, Sept. 1977

Gregson, A. and Quin, B., 'Quiet Revolution: an account of assessing at 16 plus across the whole ability range', in *Dialogue*, No. 10, Spring 1972, Schools Council Publications

Harlen, W., 'Assessing Progress by Teachers, for Teachers', *Forum* Vol. 18. No. 3

Hayes, C. and Townsend, C., 'Education and the Labour Market' in *Journal of NAIEA*, No. 8. Spring 1978

HMI, *Ten Good Schools*, Department of Education and Science, 1978

Lauwerys, J., 'Editorial' in *World Year Book of Education for 1969*

Nickse, R., 'Assessing Adult Performance', in *Higher Education Review*, Summer 1975

Nuttgens, P., *Learning to Some Purpose*, Burton Award Paper, Society of Industrial Artists and Designers, 12 Carlton House Terrace, London, SW1, 1977

Pottinger, P. S., 'Techniques and Criteria for Designing and Selecting Instruments for Assessing Teachers', in Levitov, Betty (ed.) *Licensing and Accreditation in Education*, Nebraska Curriculum Development Centre, University of Nebraska, Lincoln, Nebraska 68588, USA, 1976

Pottinger, P. S., 'Competency Assessment at School and Work', in *Social Policy* Sept./Oct. 1977

Pottinger, P. S., *Competence Testing as an Alternative to Credentials as a Basic for Licensing: Problems and Prospects* McBer, Boston, 1977

Price, C., *Prospects for Examinations*, CIS Working Paper No. 28, from Centre for Institutional Studies, North East London Polytechnic, Holbrook Road, E15

Pupils' Profile of Achievement, Helston School, Cornwall

Raven, J., 'Research Needs in Relation to Examinations, Appendix P', in *Final Report of the Committee on the Form and Function of the Intermediate Certificate Examination*, Government Publications Office, Dublin, 1975

Raven, J., 'Toward a Conceptual Framework for Thinking about Human Resources, their Assessment, Development and Consequences', in *Personnel Review 6*, 1977

Raven, J., 'School Rejection and its Amelioration', in *Educational Research*, Vol. 20, No. 1, NFER, 1977

Tinkler, G., 'Predictability of Success in CNAA First Degree Examinations', in *Journal of NAIEA*, No. 10, Spring 1979

The Attainments of the School Leaver, Minutes of Evidence taken before the Expenditure Committee (Education, Arts and Home Office Sub-Committee), Monday, 4 April, 1977, HMSO

Yates, A., *The Measurement of Productivity in Education*, a paper given to the North of England Conference, January 1976, from the Director, NFER